Success in Writing

Teacher's Resource Manual

THE PIEDMONT SCHOOL
815 Old Mill Rd.
High Point, NC 27265

GLOBE FEARON
EDUCATIONAL PUBLISHER
A Division of Simon & Schuster
Upper Saddle River, New Jersey

Executive Editor: Jean Liccione
Senior Editor: Karen Bernhaut
Project Editor: Lynn W. Kloss
Editor: Brian Hawkes
Editorial Assistant: Ryan Jones
Editorial Development: WordWise, Inc./Sandra Widener
Production Editor: Alan Dalgleish
Market Manager: Rhonda Anderson
Cover Design: Leslie Baker

Printed in the United States of America
3 4 5 6 7 8 9 10   99

ISBN 0-835-92272-3

GLOBE FEARON EDUCATIONAL PUBLISHER
A Division of Simon & Schuster
Upper Saddle River, New Jersey

CONTENTS

....

Organization of the Student Edition

Four of the *Success in Writing* books cover the different modes of writing: *Writing To Persuade* (persuasion), *Writing To Tell A Story* (narration), *Writing To Explain* (exposition), and *Writing To Describe* (description). A fifth book, *Grammar Skills for Writers*, teaches the grammar, mechanics, usage, and punctuation writers need to know.

Structure of the Books

In the books that discuss the different modes of writing, please note the following:

Unit 1 gives an overview of the particular mode of writing. Chapter 1 explains the basic structure of the writing mode. Chapter 2 emphasizes style issues relevant to each mode of writing.

Unit 2 takes students step by step through the writing process in the particular mode. Chapter 1 shows students how to plan their writing through prewriting activities. Chapter 2 helps them develop their writing through using drafts. Chapter 3 teaches students ways to complete their writing through revising, proofreading, and publishing their work.

Unit 3 contains three types of writing within a mode, such as writing a letter of complaint or summarizing a story. Each type of writing is discussed in a separate chapter.

Unit 4 has students practice writing two assignments in the mode. Chapter 1 describes the steps of writing a test essay. Chapter 2 involves a special project, for example, writing a research paper or an advertisement.

In *Grammar Skills for Writers*, please note the following:

Unit 1 discusses understanding sentence purpose and structure. Unit 2 takes students step by step through the conventions of building sentences, including grammar and mechanics. Unit 3 discusses sentence style, including ways to vary sentences, build paragraphs, and revise and edit writing. This book complements the other four books by emphasizing the ways grammar skills are used in the writing process. Students complete practice exercises, then apply the skills they've learned to their own writing.

Unit, Chapter, and Lesson Structure

The unit openers, chapter openers, and lessons all follow the same structure. They contain an introduction; then a section called either What To Do or Define It, which gives specific instructions for a task or explains a concept. Next comes either How To Do It or Understand It, which provides a model for achieving the task or applying the concept. Finally, in Review It and/or Apply It, students are asked to answer questions or complete an assignment by using the techniques or concepts discussed in that section.

All the units end with a section that asks what students have learned. This section contains questions that help students review the terms and concepts they have learned in each lesson.

Writing Guides

At the back of each book is a one-page description of the writing process. In the books that feature a mode of writing, this page is followed by A Guide for Writers: Grammar, Mechanics, and Usage for students who need to review the basics of grammar. At the back of *Grammar Skills for Writers* is A Guide for Writers: Terms to Know, which provides a mini-glossary of the terms taught and a page reference for each term.

Teacher's Resource Manual Overview

This Teacher's Resource Manual (TRM) offers suggestions for guiding students through the *Success in Writing* series. Many of the lessons in the student texts provide excellent opportunities for students to work with a partner or in a group. Strategies for cooperative learning activities are offered on page 6 and throughout the Notes and Answers section of this TRM. Strategies are also provided to help English-as-a-Second-Language students and students with limited English proficiency understand the intricacies and subtleties of the English language. A list of general activities for ESL/LEP students is found on page 7. Lesson-specific strategies are provided in the Notes and Answers section of this TRM.

The Assessment Guide offers suggestions for using various assessment methods and for helping students build portfolios of their work—from quickly jotted notes to final essays. The Assessment Guide also contains a rubric for evaluating and scoring essays written in each mode of writing, as well as sample essays written for each level of scoring.

The Notes and Answers section of this TRM contains answers and teaching strategies for the Review It and Apply It assignments. You will also find unit, chapter, and lesson notes that provide additional teaching strategies.

The Student Publications section of the TRM lists publications—both print and online—that publish student writing.

Graphic Organizers prepare students for writing and help them organize their thoughts and ideas. Organizers in which the students can write are provided throughout the modules in the Student Edition. Reproducible graphic organizers are also provided on pages 99–112 of this TRM for use with particular lessons or with any writing assignment.

Throughout the books, students are asked to evaluate each other's writing. You might want to copy and distribute the Peer-Assessment Checklist provided on page 108 of this TRM. This worksheet can help students remain focused while they evaluate each other's work.

Students might also need help in focusing on their own writing. Before students begin work on any writing assignment, you might want to hand out copies of the Student Self-Assessment Forms provided on page 107 of this TRM. Students can use these forms throughout the chapters to set goals, evaluate how well they met those goals, and decide how they might better to meet these goals in similar assignments.

The TRM ends with Writing Assessments for each mode of writing. These assessment sheets present both a well-written paragraph and a poorly written paragraph in each writing mode. Students are then asked to evaluate the two samples. This exercise can be used at the end of a unit or at the completion of a book to evaluate the students' understanding of the mode of writing.

Teaching Strategies

Cooperative Learning Strategies

During many of the writing assignments, students can work together with partners, a small group, or the entire class. The following suggestions will make cooperative learning a beneficial and successful experience for all the students involved.

- Find a way for every person in the group to have an essential role in the assignment. Conversely, do not allow any one student in a group to take on too much of the total work.

- Make the size of the group match the assignment. Use an appropriate number of group members so that all can take on a reasonable portion of the work.

- When choosing groups, avoid self-selected groups that isolate less popular students or students who are not proficient in English. Work with the students to resolve any conflicts that arise.

- Allow students to decide which tasks need to be done and who will be responsible for each. You may want to have each group member write out what he or she will accomplish during the assignment to avoid any misunderstandings.

- Periodically, check on each group's progress. Finding trouble areas while the work is in progress will lead to a more satisfying and successful result.

- Place the responsibility with the students. Make students aware of the consequences of not performing their parts. Consider assigning both an individual and a group grade.

A number of cooperative learning strategies have been provided for specific Apply It activities within the Notes and Answers section of the TRM. However, the following general activities can help facilitate the cooperative learning experience throughout the modules.

Brainstorming: Encourage students to discuss assignments and talk about possible approaches to completing them. A member of the group can summarize the ideas developed in these discussions.

Evaluating: Have students exchange and evaluate one another's work using the checklists often provided in the How To Do It section of the lessons.

Problem Solving: Have the students discuss problems they encounter while completing the assignments. Encourage them to analyze the reasons for the problems and to share problem-solving strategies.

Review: Have small groups use the What Have You Learned . . . questions for review. Encourage them to discuss their thoughts about the key elements of the unit.

ESL/LEP Strategies

English-as-a-Second-Language and Limited-English-Proficiency students face several challenges in writing. They may be unfamiliar with certain aspects of syntax, grammar rules, and idiomatic language. They also may not have the vocabulary range necessary to successfully complete an assignment, especially those assignments calling for descriptive or detailed language. Some of the ESL/LEP students may have trouble picking up on certain word cues in questions or writing prompts. The following guidelines may help you ease the ESL/LEP students' transition to fluent English and help them achieve better understanding of good writing habits.

- Read or have the students read the Review It and Apply It sections aloud. When students hear language, they can more easily grasp its meaning through emphasis and tone. Students will not be able to complete an assignment they do not fully understand.

- Have the ESL/LEP students restate the assignment in their own words to be sure of their comprehension.

- Help students define unfamiliar terms, phrases, and idioms.

- Whenever possible during assignments, pair an English-proficient student with an ESL/LEP student. Both students can gain a deeper understanding of language and writing by analyzing it in detail.

- Encourage students to use experiences from their own cultures as ideas for writing assignments, to support an opinion or argument, to provide examples, and to add details to their writing.

- Encourage students who are more comfortable thinking in their native language to do their preliminary work—graphic organizers, notes, and outlines—in that language.

Assessment Guide

Process writing often creates exciting student-centered classrooms. It can also make assessment quite challenging. However, evaluating student writing can be an opportunity rather than a chore. It can provide you with a clear record of student progress as well as telling you where students need help. Among the most effective new assessment methods are student self-assessment, peer assessment, and teacher-student writing conferences.

Student Self-Assessment

There are several ways to judge the quality of student writing. One way is to have students assess themselves. (See the reproducible masters in this TRM for the student self-assessment forms.) What are their goals for the writing assignment? Where do they think they need improvement? In some cases, students may need your help for this exercise. They may know something doesn't sound or feel right, but are unable to pinpoint why. Students can use their first assessment as a way toward writing another version of their work to be judged by you.

Peer Assessment

Peer evaluation can also be a successful method of assessment. Students work in small groups, with each student taking turns reading his or her work and receiving comments from peers about the effectiveness of the writing and where it could use improvement. (See the reproducible masters in this TRM for peer-assessment checklists.) Encourage students to be objective and constructive when they assess one another's work. You might model the evaluation procedure by making a first comment in which you point out one or two strengths of a student's work, as well as pinpointing an area that needs clarification or additional development. Modeling respect for student work can often set a tone students can easily follow.

Writing Conferences

Conferences between the teacher and the individual student enable students to express ideas and problems. Conferences also ensure clear understanding of teacher's feedback. You can use conferences to comment both on strengths and weaknesses in students' work at any point in an assignment or at any stage in the writing process. Avoid overwhelming students by keeping conferences brief and by focusing on only one or two writing problems.

Portfolio Assessment

Students' progress in their writing abilities can be enhanced by assembling portfolios of their work. Students should keep separate portfolios for each module. Portfolios should include examples from Unit 1 that will help students focus on the basic structure of a particular writing mode. The portfolios should also include the students' notes, graphic organizers, drafts, and final essays from Unit 2. These will provide the students with an easy reference guide to the step-by-step process involved in each writing mode. Any other examples of their work that have been assessed to be good representations of a phase of the writing process or of a particular mode of writing should go into the portfolios as well.

Engage students in choosing examples for inclusion in their portfolios. Making choices for their portfolios helps students develop independence and gives them pride of ownership of the work that they do.

By looking through the examples in their portfolios at regular intervals, students can review their progress and evaluate their development as writers. Students can also look back at their notes and graphic organizers from earlier lessons if they are having problems with their current assignments.

These portfolios will also be useful to you in evaluating the progress of the students' writing skills. They will assist you in assessing students' understanding of key ideas and in monitoring their progress. As you look at student work with an eye to assessing it, look at first drafts of student work as works in progress. Your nonjudgmental comments can provide a chance for students to see the possibility for improvement in their work. In a rough draft, first look at the ideas; then execution. By the time students have turned in their final drafts, assessment can occur on a number of levels, from ideas to mechanics. The scoring guides that follow list factors to look for as you assess student writing.

How To Score A Persuasive Essay

The following reflects the kind of persuasive essay that students will be asked to write in the units of the *Writing To Persuade* module. The essays are based on the following prompt:

Some members of the History Club want to spend the club fund on a big end-of-the-year party. Other members want to spend the fund on a day-long trip to the Smithsonian Museum. Which would you choose and why?

The essays on pages 11-14 are examples of student writing. The essays are scored on a scale of 1 to 4, with 4 being the best score. They are scored according to the following criteria:

A. Responses that represent the highest standard receive an evaluation of 4. The response is clearly focused on the prompt. Reasons are presented convincingly with well-chosen support for the position chosen. The organization is clear and consistent and has a coherent sense of completeness. Introductory, transitional, and concluding elements contribute to a well-organized progression. Word choice is appropriate and varied, and sentence structure is interesting. Minor mechanical errors do not interfere with the understanding of the essay.

B. Responses that represent good efforts receive an evaluation of 3. The response focuses on the prompt. Reasons are limited, but well supported, or they are ample and moderately supported. In some cases, only one reason is provided, but the support for that reason is extensive and well elaborated. Organization is logical, but has minor gaps or divergences. Word choice is effective; there are transitions between ideas; and there has been an effort to vary sentence structure. Mechanical errors are present, but they do not affect the understanding of the essay.

C. Responses that are minimally successful receive an evaluation of 2. The response answers the prompt and remains on the topic throughout. Reasons are provided without elaboration, or there is only one sketchily elaborated reason provided in support of the argument chosen. Organizational structure is confusing and inconsistent. The word choice is limited, and sentence structure is repetitive. Errors in mechanics impair the understanding of the essay.

D. Responses that are unsuccessful receive an evaluation of 1. The response does not answer the prompt, or addresses the question in a skeletal way and does not remain on the topic. There is minimal support of the position chosen and/or the reasons presented do not relate to the position taken. The language is confusing, and the sentence structure is repetitive. Errors in usage, mechanics, and spelling impede the reader's understanding of the essay.

Further elaboration of the scoring can be found in the paragraphs following each essay. Though not shown extensively in the samples, essays scoring 2 and 1 generally will contain numerous spelling, grammar, and punctuation errors.

Essay One: Score of 4

How many of the students in my class have been to a party? Probably, all of them. How many have been to the most interesting museum in the world—the Smithsonian? Very few, I've discovered. A visit to the Smithsonian would be the best use of our History Club dues. The museum trip would be of special interest to club members. It would provide them with a unique opportunity to learn more about history. Most importantly, however, it would be fun for everyone.

This year, our club has spent much of its time discussing the fiftieth anniversary of the bombing of Hiroshima and the end of World War II. The Smithsonian is running a special exhibit on exactly this subject. Rather than just talk about what happened, we would be able to read first-hand accounts, see American soldiers' memorabilia, examine photographs of the event that have never been shown before, and see the Enola Gay. We have a chance to view pieces of the most dramatic historical events with our own eyes.

Other parts of the museum have many exhibits that also show pieces of history. There are exhibits focusing on Native Americans' roles in history, on the civil rights movement, and on the political roles of our country's First Ladies. These exhibits can help answer some questions that members have had about certain historical events. They will also provide us with many new topics for discussion during next year's History Club meetings.

Most of all, a trip to the Smithsonian would be a fun experience. There are exhibits that appeal to all members of our club. The club members already enjoy spending time with other students with common interests. We would have an opportunity to spend an entire day together, talking about and viewing our favorite subject—history.

Students can attend parties anytime. Visiting the Smithsonian will be an educational and enjoyable way to spend our class funds. I urge other members of the club to choose the museum visit. A trip to the museum will be remembered as a highlight of our school experience.

The introductory paragraph of this essay focuses on the prompt and clearly states the writer's opinion. The paragraph also broadly outlines the reasons the writer will present for holding that opinion. Reasons are presented in an organized manner and examples are provided to support each reason. The organization is coherent with a clearly delineated introduction, body, and conclusion. Sentence structure is varied and interesting.

Essay Two: Score of 3

A trip to the Smithsonian would be a better idea than having a party. We should use the funds for the trip. We can always go to a party. However, most of us have never been to such a huge and interesting museum. The museum has a special exhibit on Hiroshima. Our club spent a lot of time talking about the bombing. We'd all enjoy seeing exhibits about it. This part of the museum would help us learn more about the end of World War II.

The Smithsonian also has exhibits on other historical subjects. One contains all the First Ladies' inaugural dresses. Museums have many kinds of things that you can't see anywhere else. I especially like the kinds of museums that have preserved animals from around the world. I know I would like the Smithsonian museum as well. The better choice for the use of our club funds is the museum trip.

The writer gives a clear and specific answer to the prompt in the first paragraph. While the development of the argument is generally logical in the first paragraph, it becomes uneven in the second paragraph. The digression about other museums weakens the organization and flow. Although some reasons are given to support the writer's opinion, elaboration is weak. More substantial reasons would have also been helpful in getting the writer's opinion across to the reader.

Essay Three: Score of 2

Parties usually are fun. Museums are boring so I don't like them. Mostly, you just walk around looking at old stuff. Alot of it is ugly. We should have a party. We can get lots of food and things to drink but not beer. Kids shouldn't drink alcohol it ruins your life.

Everyone would enjoy a party. Decorating for a party is fun and so is eating alot of food. We can have a theme party like the discovery of america or the end of world war 2 or something else. That is why I would rather have a party.

The first and second sentences are somewhat related to the prompt in that the writer compares parties with going to a museum. The writer does not address the prompt's question about how the club funds should be used, but does show a preference between the choices. However, the reader needs to do a certain amount of guessing to infer the writer's position on the subject. The writer does not give reasons or facts to support the opinion, and references to alcohol are disruptive. Because the paper is short, there is not much to organize. However, the organization is somewhat logical, though off the intended subject.

Essay Four: Score of 1

Lets have a history club party. I really like parties. I had a really good party once. All my friends came and brang me present. The best present was a game you can play on the tv. The two little men chase a gorilla up and down. I always win my brother because he is too young. I laugh at the funny men sometimes.

The first sentence answers the prompt. However, the essay immediately drifts from the central idea. There are no details to support the opinion given in the first sentence. Most of the essay has nothing to do with the prompt. The essay is too short to be organized. Thoughts included are unrelated and nearly unintelligible.

How To Score A Narrative Essay

The following reflects the kind of essay that students will be asked to write in the units of the *Writing To Tell A Story* module. The essays are based on the following prompts:

Do you remember the first time you ever stayed away from home overnight? Write an essay that tells the story of that experience.

The essays on pages 16-19 are examples of student writing. The essays are scored on a scale of 1 to 4, with 4 being the best score, according to the following criteria:

A. Responses that represent the highest standard receive an evaluation of 4. The response answers the prompt. The narrative is well organized and has a clear sequence of events with a beginning, middle, and end. A recognizable time frame is established, and the events that occur happen within that time frame. Each paragraph has a clearly defined, well-elaborated main idea. Ideas flow smoothly with coherence and clarity. Sentence structure is varied and interesting; word choice is intelligent. Minor errors in spelling and mechanics do not impair understanding of the essay.

B. Responses that represent good efforts receive an evaluation of 3. The response focuses on the prompt. The organization is reasonable, and events are described in their actual sequence. Events are introduced but unevenly described, or one event is extensively elaborated, while others are only listed or absent. Word choice is intelligent, and sentence structure is interesting. Minor errors in conventions do not interfere with understanding of the essay.

C. Responses that are minimally successful receive an evaluation of 2. The response is appropriate to the prompt. However, the organization is confusing; events are described without attention to the order in which they occur, making the essay difficult to follow. The time frame is vaguely defined. The essay remains focused on the topic, but details are few and presented without elaboration. Word choice is repetitive; sentence structure is without variety. Errors in spelling and mechanics impede understanding of the essay.

D. Responses that are unsuccessful receive an evaluation of 1. The response minimally addresses the prompt. Organization is incoherent. Events are represented out of order, or inappropriate events are included. The writer gives examples unconnected to the topic. Word choice is limited and often inappropriate; sentence structure is repetitive or incorrect. Errors in spelling, grammar, and mechanics seriously interfere with understanding of the essay.

Further elaboration of the scoring can be found in the paragraphs following each essay. Though not shown extensively in the samples, essays scoring 2 and 1 generally will contain numerous spelling, grammar, and punctuation errors.

Essay One: Score of 4

I remember secretly tucking *Baby Wet 'n' Cry* into the bottom of my overnight bag. I was sure I was old enough for my first sleepover at my friend Pammy's house. However, I did not feel grown-up enough to leave behind this small bit of childhood security. I covered the doll with my bathrobe and zipped the bag closed.

I heard my dad call me to get ready to leave. I pulled on my coat, grabbed my bag, and headed for the front door. Because it was already dark, my father insisted on walking me from our house to Pammy's, two doors away. I was excited, happy, nervous, and a little frightened all at once.

When we got to my neighbor's house, Pammy was standing at the door. My father kissed me goodnight, told me not to get homesick, and then left. Pammy and I went straight to her bedroom, which was always very neat. She even arranged her dolls on a shelf by name in alphabetical order.

For the rest of the evening, we played every game in her toy closet. Of course, these also had to be removed and replaced in alphabetical order. I got a odd feeling in my stomach when I thought of the games my two sisters were probably playing at home.

Nonetheless, I continued to play and chatter away with Pammy. Eventually her mother came in to say it was bedtime. We changed into our pajamas, brushed our teeth, and climbed into the top bunk together. We continued our chatter until her father came in and sent Pammy into the lower bunk. She promptly fell asleep.

Alone now and still awake, I felt that odd twinge in my stomach again. I couldn't stop thinking about what my sisters and parents were doing while I was gone. Were they all sitting together in the den watching TV? Were they in the kitchen having a snack? Nighttime snacks weren't allowed at Pammy's house.

As I wondered whether my mom was tucking my sisters into bed, tears began to roll down my checks. I wanted to go home. I began to cry harder, sobbing loudly enough to wake Pammy and bring her father into the room. Between sobs, I expressed my desire to return home—now.

Pammy's father silently walked me home. I openly clutched my doll to my chest as we walked. When we reached my house Pammy's father informed me that I would not be invited to sleep over again until I was much older. I didn't mind.

The narrative is well organized with a clear beginning, middle, and end. The events are presented in a recognizable sequence and the transitional phrases nicely establish the time frame. Each paragraph is about a specific point in time. There is a consistent point of view and a clear voice throughout. The writer's choice of language helps the reader identify with the homesick child in the story. Sentence structure is interesting and varied in construction and length.

Essay Two: Score of 3

The first time I ever stayed away from home was the time my mother went to the hospital to have my younger brother. I spent the night at my grandmother's house across town. The first thing I remember is being woken at what seemed to me the middle of the night. It was probably more like nine o'clock.

My parent's had already left. I realized it was my grandmother who had woken me. I was too sleepy to see her clearly, but I smelled the familiar scent of lilacs in the room. My grandmother always smelled of lilacs. Grandma carried me out to her car since I had not woken up enough to walk. By the time we reached her house I was wide awake.

Once inside the house, I had a million questions for my grandmother. I wanted to know how long I would be staying, when would the baby be born, when I could see it, would it be a boy, and on and on. Finally, my grandmother made me stop talking. We had cookies and orange juice. Most people have milk with their cookies but there wasn't any milk because my grandmother doesn't like it.

I fell asleep on her scratchy, throw-pillow covered couch. When I woke up the next morning, my father was already there. He told me that I had a new baby brother. I couldn't wait to get home to see him.

The narrative answers the prompt. The essay maintains a strong focus. The events are presented in a clear, logical order, digressing briefly at the end of the third paragraph. It has a strong concluding sentence. However, the writer uses few supporting details. A transition, such as *eventually*, would be helpful in the first sentence of the fourth paragraph.

Essay Three: Score of 2

My first night away from home was spent at a friend's house. This friend was from school. We were in the second grade together. She didn't live near me so my mother drove me to her house. It wasn't dark yet, so we played outside for awhile. Then it was getting dark so we went inside.

I liked this friend a lot she was very sweet. Sometimes she would share her lunch with me when I didn't like mine. My mother gave me peanut butter and jelly sandwiches a lot that I don't like when I was little or even now.

My friend and me played inside her house in the den. She had a new game that I had never played before. It was chutes and ladder. It was really fun so we played it again and again. Then it was time to go to sleep. So we did. Before we went to sleep, her mother called us into the kitchen for a snack. We had potato chips and soda. I had a lot of fun on my first sleepover.

The first sentence of the essay is appropriate to the prompt. The first paragraph is focused on the subject. However, the following paragraph is rambling and completely off the subject. Overall, the organization is confusing, and events are presented out of sequence. The writer does convey the events of a first sleepover, though not coherently. Word choices are dull, and details are lacking.

Essay Four: Score of 1

I sleep at my friend's house all the time. My father travels a lot so I like the company. My friends parent are really nice they like to have me stay with them. Usually I sleep in my friends room. I do my homework with my friend we finish quick then we play. I like to get a lot of sleep.

The writer misses the point of the prompt, writing an essay on sleeping at a friend's house in the present. The essay is poorly written and unorganized. The sentences are disconnected. The events are out of order and confusing.

How To Score An Expository Essay

The following reflects the kind of expository essay that students will be asked to write in the units of the *Writing To Explain* module. The essays are based on the following prompt:

Think about something that you've made or built, such as a painting, a soap box racer, or a favorite meal. Explain to someone else how they could make or build the same thing.

The essays on pages 21-24 are examples of student writing. The essays are scored on a scale of 1 to 4, with 4 being the best score according to the following criteria:

A. Responses that represent the highest standard receive an evaluation of 4. The essay addresses the topic, has a thesis statement, supporting details, and a conclusion. The essay never strays from the thesis. The information is organized clearly and logically; explanations, ideas, or steps in a process are easy to follow. Each paragraph has a clearly defined, well-developed idea as exemplified by details, examples, or reasons that support the thesis. Language is intelligent and imaginative. Spelling and mechanical errors are rare and do not impair understanding.

B. Responses that represent good efforts receive an evaluation of 3. The writer answers the prompt and stays focused throughout the essay. The information is organized in a logical and clear order, but minor digressions from the main idea may be present. Supporting details develop most of the ideas presented. However, some ideas may have insufficient or no supporting details. Sentence structure and word choice are appropriate and intelligent. Errors in spelling and mechanics do not interfere with understanding.

C. Responses that are minimally successful receive an evaluation of 2. The response is appropriate to the prompt and remains focused on the central idea. Nevertheless, organization is poor and confusing. Explanations, ideas, or steps in a process are not presented in a logical order. Ideas are presented with limited or no supporting details. The writer may digress from the central idea. Language and sentence structure are repetitive and unimaginative. Errors in spelling and mechanics make the essay difficult to understand.

D. Responses that are unsuccessful receive an evaluation of 1. The response minimally answers the prompt, but lacks a plan of organization. The writer digresses from the central idea and does not maintain a clear focus throughout the essay. Examples, ideas, or supporting details are rare and may be inappropriate or unconnected to the topic. Word choice is limited and repetitious. The essay demonstrates a lack of paragraph or sentence structure. Spelling, grammatical, and mechanical errors seriously impair understanding.

Further elaboration of the scoring can be found in the paragraphs following each essay. Though not shown extensively in the samples, essays scoring 2 and 1 generally will contain numerous spelling, grammar, and punctuation errors.

Essay One: Score of 4

Painting with watercolors is my favorite activity. It can be very rewarding and relaxing. If you would like to learn to use watercolors, there are a number of steps you must follow.

First, you need to gather the right supplies. The best materials for painting can be found in an art supplies or crafts store. You will need a box of watercolor paints containing tubes of these six colors: blue, red, yellow, green, purple, and orange. These colors can be mixed to obtain any other hue you will want. You will need two or three paint brushes of different widths and a mixing palette. You will also need a book of paper meant especially for use with watercolors. You should also buy blocking tape. This is made of paper with a gluey backing.

Once you've gotten the supplies, you need to prepare the paper. Soak a sheet of paper in cool water. When the paper is thoroughly wetted, smooth it out on a flat, movable surface. Preferably, you should use a wooden easel. Place strips of blocking tape around all four edges to hold the paper in place. Then, let the paper dry. This will keep the paper from wrinkling when you apply the watercolors.

Finally, it is time to decide on a subject. After you've chosen what you will paint, fill a small cup with clear water. Then squeeze out a little of the color paint you would like to start with. Dip your brush in the water. Next, dab it gently in the paint; you do not need very much.

Now begin painting your subject. Watercolor should be applied lightly to the paper. The intent is to let some of the white of the paper show through the paint. Continue to squeeze out little dabs of paint as you need it.

Practice these steps for a few weeks and you may be on your way to a wonderful career, or at least an enjoyable hobby, as an artist.

The essay answers the prompt, introducing the central idea in the first paragraph. Each paragraph explains a step in the process—gathering supplies, preparing the paper, and finally, painting. The writer clearly and completely explains how each step is accomplished. The process is presented in a logical order, couched in language that is easy to follow. The sentence structure is simple and to the point.

Essay Two: Score of 3

Making a terrarium is fun and simple. These are the steps you need to follow to make one yourself.

You will need a 2-liter soda bottle, sand, ground up charcoal, and soil. You can get the soil from outside. You should also gather small plants, including their roots, from outside.

Cut the neck off the soda bottle. Also snap off the hard plastic base. Save this because you will need it later.

Pour the sand into the bottom of the bottle. Then pour in some charcoal. Next, pour a layer of sand on top of the charcoal. Finally, add just enough water to moisten the soil.

Use a thin stick to poke holes in the soil. Plant the plants in the holes. Pat the soil around the plants to be sure they are in firmly.

Fit the plastic base over the top of the bottle. Use tape to make a solid seal. You don't want the water to escape. Your terrarium is now complete.

The essay is focused on the prompt throughout. The process is well defined; the organization is sensible. The writer does not give the specific amounts or proportions of sand, charcoal, or gravel to be used. Word choice is clear, but sometimes confusing (using two meanings of *plant* in the same sentence). Sentence structure is generally appropriate. The student could have made better use of transitional words and phrases to smooth the flow of the essay.

Essay Three: Score of 2

This is how you can build a bird house like I did. Take four peaces of wood to make the four sides of the birdhouse. Use a router bit to drill a big hole in one peace of wood for the birds to get in. Drill a smaller hole to put a dowel in for a perch for the bird to sit on. Hammer in nails to hold the sides together. Make sure their square or the bottom wont fit right.

Take another peace of wood and nail it to the bottom of the other peaces of wood. Then nail the top peace of wood on. This bird house has a flat roof. My neighbor has a blue and red birdhouse with a pointed roof. Then you can paint the bird house. Then nail the birdhouse to a branch in a tree.

The essay addresses the prompt in the introductory paragraph. Confusing organization and lack of specific information on the size of the pieces of wood and drill bits creates difficulty in following the process. However, in the first paragraph the writer does attempt to present the steps in some kind of order. In the second paragraph, the repetitive use of the transition *then* adds nothing to the flow of the essay and, in fact, detracts from it. The comment about the neighbor's birdhouse is also distracting. The sentences are either choppy or run on.

Essay Four: Score of 1

I would like to water ski. I watched it on tv shows. A boat pulls you on them. You use two skis sometimes one. Once somebody skied with their teeth on a rope instead of their hands. I want to too. Its really cool when peeple crash. Their flying off the ramps falling in the water.

The writer does not address the prompt. Instead, an attempt is made at explaining something the writer would like to do but has not. The writer does manage to list a rudimentary step or two involved in water skiing. Because the essay is so short, there is little to organize. However, the writer's attempt at organization is confusing and incoherent. Sentences are poorly constructed.

How To Score a Descriptive Essay

The following reflects the kind of essay that students will be asked to write in the units of the Writing To Describe module. The essays are based on the following prompt:

Imagine that you've won a family weekend vacation to a fancy hotel in a large city or to a rustic inn far out in the country. Write an essay that describes the hotel or inn and your feelings for your surroundings.

The essays on pages 26-29 are examples of student writing. The essays are scored on a scale of 1 to 4, with 4 being the best score. They are scored according to the following criteria:

A. Responses that represent the highest standard receive an evaluation of 4. The response answers the prompt by clearly describing someone or something and does not stray from this central idea. The organization demonstrates logical progression and overall completeness. Descriptions are couched in vivid sensory language and rich detail, bringing images to life. Ideas flow smoothly with coherence and clarity. Sentence structure is interesting, and word choice is intelligent. Minor errors in spelling and mechanics do not impair understanding.

B. Responses that represent good efforts receive an evaluation of 3. The response focuses on the prompt and does not wander from the item being described. Either many details are given but are unevenly elaborated, or one detail is extensively elaborated, while others are only listed or absent. The organization is generally logical with one or two gaps. Word choice is intelligent, but not evocative. Sentence structure is interesting, and minor errors in conventions do not interfere with understanding.

C. Responses that are minimally successful receive an evaluation of 2. The response answers the prompt, staying with one central idea. Details are presented without elaboration and are not always relevant to the topic. The organization is minimal and confusing. Word choice is repetitive and without attention to sensory imagery. Sentence structure lacks variety. Errors in spelling and mechanics impede understanding.

D. Responses that are unsuccessful receive an evaluation of 1. The response addresses the prompt, without providing descriptive details to elaborate on the response. The essay wanders off the topic and is difficult to understand. Organization is confused and incoherent. Word choice is limited and not descriptive in nature; sentence structure is awkward and repetitive. Errors in spelling, grammar, and mechanics seriously interfere with understanding.

Further elaboration of the scoring can be found in the paragraphs following each essay. Though not shown extensively in the samples, essays scoring 2 and 1 generally will contain numerous spelling, grammar, and punctuation errors.

Essay One: Score of 4

I couldn't believe my luck. I almost never enter contests, but this one seemed too tempting—an entire weekend away from the noisy, crowded city. I simply filled out a form to have a chance at winning a relaxing family weekend at the Friend's Country Inn. I still can't believe that I won! But there we were on Friday evening, pulling up in front of the most beautiful old Victorian mansion.

Round, pointed turrets jutted out here and there from the roof. A white-painted porch wrapped around the house like a comforting old quilt. Fairy-tale gingerbread carvings of hearts and birds and scrolls accented the building from porch to roof. I hadn't even entered the building and already, every muscle in my body relaxed.

As we walked inside, we were met by the smell of fresh bread baking. The Inn is famous for its cooking, especially the fluffy, air-filled popovers. The sharp pain in my stomach reminded me I hadn't had anything but a small bowl of cereal that morning. However, my hunger would have to wait until I'd settled in.

The porter led us to our rooms on the third story. The narrow, winding stair-case was so steep I had to lift my knees almost to my waste to climb each step. I was grateful to have the porter carrying my bags.

My room was in one of the turrets. I found the roundness of the walls and the curve of the ceiling soothing, as if I were inside a warm cocoon. The rosewood moldings shone decades of dusting and polishing. I admired the colorful patch-work quilt covering the down-filled mattress of my antique bed. It was then that my whole family decided to order room service rather than leave the comfort of our quarters.

While eating, I sat by the open window, breathing in the sweet scent of the surrounding pine trees. Upon finishing my meal, I snuggled beneath the covers. The flannel of my pajamas wrapped my body in warmth and softness. I was asleep quickly, falling into the gentle sleep of a newborn child in its mother's arms.

The writer clearly focuses on the prompt in the introductory paragraph. The description of the inn is detailed; the writer's choice of words makes the inn real for the readers. The strong sensory images provide a vivid description of the surroundings and the mood of calmness they evoked in the writer. The essay is well organized, possessing a clear beginning, middle, and end. Sentences are properly constructed.

Essay Two: Score of 3

The best thing that ever happened to me was winning a family trip to the Sherman Hotel in New York City. It is the most beautiful and luxurious place I have ever been in my life. I felt so comfortable and pampered that I never wanted to leave.

The hotel itself is elaborately decorated, inside and out. The entrance is made of carved, pink granite including two regal lions on either side. The shiny marble steps lead into a lobby covered with an expansive oriental rug. The rug is mostly pale blue with an intricate floral design.

Our suite was also beautiful. It had a small living room where you walked in. Off to one side were the large bedrooms. I had a king sized bed all to myself. Both rooms had ornate marble fireplaces. The marble was as smooth as ice. We never had time to use them though. Fresh flowers with a wonderful scent were flowing out of antique vases on the mantles.

The furnishings were delicate antiques. I don't know what kind. One of the chairs looked so fragile I was afraid to sit in it.

Being in those surroundings made me feel like I was as rich as the paying guests. I'll go back someday when I really am.

The prompt is answered in the introductory paragraph. Descriptive details are provided in subsequent paragraphs. However, the details could be more specific and elaborate. Also, the writer does not use the details to give the reader a sense of his feelings. Each paragraph in the body begins with a specific idea, which is given elaboration in the remainder of the paragraph. The essay is well structured, and the organization is clear. Sentences are interesting though brief, giving the essay a choppy feel. Word choices are adequate.

Essay Three: Score of 2

I won a family trip to a country inn far away from the city. It was very big it had a lot of rooms. It was painted a light blue so that it matched the sky.

The inn was at the top of a mountain. On the way we passed through some other high mountains to get there. Driving over them was like being on a rollercoaster I really like them.

I had to go around and around the stairs to get to my room. My room was above the porch that went around the whole building. The room was round with a pointy ceiling. Lite came in in the mornings.

I enjoyed being there it was quiet. We spent time as a family noone else bothered us all weekend.

The writer answers the part of the prompt that asks for a description of the inn. However, the writer's feelings are not described. The description of the inn matching the sky is an interesting image. There writer digresses from the topic by mentioning the mountains. Also, you can't be sure whether the writer likes the mountains or roller coasters. Most of the details are vague and incomplete. The organization is somewhat logical, though the run-on sentences interfere with understanding.

Essay Four: Score of 1

The hotel in the city is very nice. There were a bunch of other people there too. The rooms are nice and big. Its not like my house mine is small and I dont have my own room. My sister is always bugging me borrows my stuff that gets broke.

The first three sentences minimally respond to the prompt. The essay provides no details or any useful descriptions. The remainder of the essay is unrelated to the topic. The sentence structure is confused, and the choice of wording is poor.

General Lesson Plan

The following guidelines can help you focus students on the purpose and intent of each unit, chapter, and lesson. It is recommended that you preread all student lessons before presenting them to the class. You may also want to review the unit, chapter, or lesson notes and strategies in this Teacher's Resource Manual (TRM).

Opening the Unit

Have students read the opener's introductory paragraph. Suggest that they brainstorm ideas on what the unit is about. Ask them "warm-up" questions to help them begin thinking about ways to approach the types of writing or editing they will do in the coming chapters.

Give students an overview of what they will learn in each chapter. Let them know what activities or projects they will be expected to complete. You might have students read the unit opener to themselves or you might read each section aloud to the class yourself before students complete the assignment in the Review It or Apply It section.

Opening the Chapter

Before beginning the chapter, you might want to copy and distribute any graphic organizers students will need, plus the peer- and self-assessment worksheets from the back of this TRM. Again, use warm-up questions to focus students on the kind of writing or editing they will be doing in the chapter.

After reading the chapter opener, students should fill in the goal-setting section of their self-assessment. You might also want to divide students into the groups for the cooperative learning exercises.

Focusing the Unit, Chapter, or Lesson

Because all of the unit openers, chapter openers, and lessons are organized in the same manner, you can use the same general approach to leading your class through them.

1. Ask students questions about how they would approach the task described in What to Do or Define It.
2. After reading How to Do It or Understand It, encourage students to ask questions about any steps they do not understand. You might also want to assess students' understanding by having them explain the steps in their own words.
3. Tell students to reread any explanation or description in How to Do It or Understand It before answering questions in Review It or Apply It. Lead a class discussion on how the Apply It assignment can be successfully completed. Again, encourage students to ask about any question or part of the assignment they do not understand. Think of your own questions to ask the class to help them successfully complete Review It or Apply It.

Closing the Lesson

You might decide to have students assess their own or each other's progress before they move from one lesson to the next. You might also check their progress yourself. Often students must successfully complete one assignment if they are to be successful on subsequent assignments. Give students time to discuss among themselves how they might better handle parts of the assignment with which they had difficulty.

Closing the Chapter

Ask students to sum up—in a discussion, in writing, or in a graphic concept map—the basic concepts of the chapter. As with the lessons, give students time to discuss how they might improve their performance of the assignments. You might want to use either written or oral review questions similar to the end-of-unit questions to see how well students have understood the concepts in the chapter.

If the objective of the chapter was to complete a final draft of a writing assignment, have students fill out a peer assessment worksheet for that project. Students can then fill in the rest of their self-assessment to evaluate how well they've met their goals and to decide where they need more practice.

Closing the Unit

Lead a discussion to help students make the links among the lessons that lead to an understanding of the overall goal of the unit.

The end-of-unit questions provide an excellent opportunity for review. Have the students answer them in class. Lead a discussion of the students' answers to each question. To improve their overall understanding of the unit's topics, you might ask students to create lists of questions to ask one another.

Notes and Answers: Writing to Persuade

UNIT 1 Understanding Persuasion

Apply It
The items on students' lists will vary but may include: convince people to change their minds on an issue; help an undecided person form an opinion on an issue; motivate someone to take action; and clearly express their opinions.

Chapter 1
Building an Argument
Review It
The three parts of a persuasive piece of writing are the introduction, the body, and the conclusion.

Lesson 1
Review It
1. *The school library does not have any news magazines.*
2. *The library should subscribe to some, so that we know what is going on in the world.*
3. *Today's students need more information than television gives them!*

Lesson 2
Review It
1. In the opening scene, Indiana Jones finds a golden statue, outsmarts a traitor, and escapes from a collapsing cave. After a villain steals the statue, Jones must outrun men who are shooting arrows at him. He then escapes in a sea plane.
2. Indiana Jones escapes a tomb filled with dangerous snakes, tricks a large group of villains, and outwits a sneaky monkey.

ESL/LEP STRATEGY: A misunderstanding of subtle language differences may be an impediment to ESL/LEP students in telling fact from opinion. Before the lesson, have the ESL/LEP students underline the unfamiliar words and phrases in the essay fragments from How to Do It on p. 8 of the student book and from Review It on p. 9 of the student book. Either you or another student can help them define these unfamiliar words.

Lesson 3
Review It
1. *Bike helmets can save lives.*
2. *Therefore, wear a helmet!*
3. *Your life is too important to risk serious injury.*
4. *These examples prove that learning a foreign language is important.*
5. *Support the teaching of languages in school, and take a foreign language class yourself.*
6. *You will become a good citizen—not only of your own country, but of the world.*

Chapter 2
Persuading with Style
Apply It
Have students identify which of the four ways to create a persuasive style is used in each of the articles they collect.

COOPERATIVE LEARNING STRATEGY: Divide the class into four groups. Assign each group one of the four ways to create a persuasive style. Within each group, have the students compare the articles they have collected that use their assigned method. Have them compile a list of common elements found in all the articles. As you go through each lesson in this chapter, have the group assigned the corresponding topic read their list to the rest of the class.

Lesson 1
Review It
1. *Our class can raise a lot of money for the annual trip at Saturday's car wash.*
2. *Join your friends at the car wash and have fun!*
3. *The weather will be hot, but the water will be cool, so you can cool off while you work!*

Lesson 2
Review It
The sentences that state an opinion are: *That's really dumb; They should be allowed to wear caps that support their favorite teams; They should be able to wear them in school, too.*

Students' answers will vary, but some facts

they may list are: By wearing baseball caps instead of fussing with a hairstyle, students save time in the morning. By wearing the caps that support their favorite teams, students feel better about themselves. Some students are anxious about their appearance; baseball caps make them look better. Wearing baseball caps has no effect on the students' learning processes, so whether a student chooses to wear a cap should not be the school's concern.

Lesson 3
Apply It
Students' Venn diagrams will vary depending on the subject chosen. Each diagram should include concise statements of the student's views in one circle, opposing views in the other circle, and views that the student and readers have in common within the intersection of the two circles.

Lesson 4
Apply It
Students' paragraphs will vary but should include a statement of one opposing opinion, a statement of their own view, and facts supporting their argument against the opposing view.

WHAT HAVE YOU LEARNED IN UNIT 1?
1. Writing to persuade gives you the opportunity to express your opinions and change people's minds.
2. You must include an introduction, a body, and a conclusion.
3. Naming of the topic, a statement of your opinion on the topic, and a sentence or sentences to get the reader involved belong in the introduction.
4. One or more paragraphs that give facts and reasons to support your opinion belong in the body of the persuasive essay.
5. The conclusion needs one paragraph that restates your opinion, urges the reader to agree with you, and ends with a positive

statement. The conclusion may sometimes include a statement that tells the reader what action to take.
6. Appeal to readers' interests and feelings; use facts that support your opinion; show respect for your readers and their views; consider the opposing views, and answer objections before they can be made.
7. You can sell your views by making the reader willing to listen by considering what your reader wants and needs.
8. Opinions cannot be proven. Facts can. A reader can disagree with your opinion, but cannot disagree with your facts.
9. Readers will be more willing to listen and agree with you if they feel you respect them and their opinions. They will also be more willing to agree with you if they see that you share some views with them.
10. By thinking about the opposing views beforehand, you can address them before the reader can object.

UNIT NOTE:
Direct the students to use their answers to questions 5-10 of What Have You Learned as a starting point of a discussion with their group or partner. Have them make a list of "Five Ways to Persuade a Reader."

Have the group choose a representative. (If students are working with partners, group several pairs together to choose a representative.) The representatives can get together to compile a master list of ways to persuade to present to the class. They may choose to use more than five choices.

UNIT 2 Writing to Persuade

Apply It

If the students are working individually, have them write down their thoughts as they imagine each step. To help the students focus on the planning stage of writing persuasion, ask them to think about such questions as: How would they decide on the topic? Who do they think the intended audience is? Why would they write about such a topic? Where would they gather the facts they would need to use in their writing? How might they organize their argument?

Chapter 1
Planning Your Writing
Apply It

Remind students at the end of each lesson to return to this list.

Lesson 1
Apply It

You may want to go over the topics that each student has identified and guide students in selecting topics with which they can work successfully throughout the rest of the chapter. They are going to need to write several ideas about their topics before narrowing the focus. They will need to identify the audiences for whom they will be writing and the goals of their writing. They will need to gather facts to support their opinions.

You also may want to narrow students' focus to topics in a certain subject area, such as school activities, the environment, their community, and so on.

Lesson 2
Apply It

When evaluating the idea webs, be sure that the reasons stated in the circle are reasonably related to the central idea. Again, you may want to guide the students in their selections of narrowed topics.

Lesson 3
Apply It

Check that students have identified appropriate audiences for their essays. Ask students to explain their final choice of an audience.

Lesson 4
Apply It

Students' answers will vary but should address each of the three questions. Evaluate how clearly and strongly they state their opinions. Also evaluate how well the facts support the students' opinions. Note whether the actions they suggest are reasonable.

ESL/LEP STRATEGY: The ESL/LEP students can practice their spoken English by leading a mini-debate. Pair an ESL/LEP student with a small group of students that are proficient in English. Have the ESL/LEP students present their opinions. Have the English-proficient students present opposing views with some reasons to support them. The ESL/LEP students can then attempt to counter the opposing views with facts and reasons of their own.

Lesson 5
Apply It

Encourage students to find and use sources other than those listed. Additional sources can include experts on their chosen topics, historians, and professional or scientific journals related to their topics. Review good note-taking techniques.

Lesson 6
Apply It

Students' planning charts will vary depending on their topics. However, they should follow the general organization described in What to Do and shown in the sample chart in How to Do It on p. 27 of the student book.

Chapter 2
Developing Your Writing
Apply It

Remind students at the end of each lesson to return to this list.

CHAPTER NOTES: Keep in mind that in each lesson of this chapter, the students have been told not to be concerned with grammar and spelling. Getting ideas down on paper is their primary goal in this activity.

Some students may have trouble with writing an introduction in Lesson 1. These students are urged to move on to Lesson 2, write the body of the essay, then return to the introduction. This method can help the students clarify their opinions and produce a stronger, more coherent topic statement.

Though a checklist is provided to evaluate the quality of the students' writing in each lesson of this chapter, keep in mind that they are writing *drafts* of their essays. The students are given the opportunity to refine their essays in the following chapter.

Lesson 1
Apply It

Students' introductions will vary but a well-written essay should: (1) begin with a topic sentence that grabs the readers' attention—the hook; (2) be followed by a statement of the student's opinion on the topic; and (3) end with a plausible reason for holding that opinion.

Lesson 2
Apply It

The body of the students' essays will vary but a well-written essay will include the following: (1) facts, examples, or reasons that support their opinions and increase in importance as the essay progresses, with the strongest fact or reason presented last; (2) an appeal to readers' interests and feelings; and (3) consideration of the opposing views and answers to objections before they can be made.

Lesson 3
Apply It

The conclusions of the students' essays will vary but a well-written essay should include: (1) a restatement of the opinion presented in the introductory paragraph; (2) a prompt for the audience to agree with the opinion or take action; and (3) a strong positive statement that draws the essay to a close. The conclusion should be brief and to the point.

Chapter 3
Completing Your Writing
Apply It

Remind students at the end of each lesson to return to this list.

Lesson 1
Apply It

Use the checklist provided for the students on p. 35 of the student book and the Assessment Guide on pp. 9-14 of the TRM to evaluate the students' essays.

ESL/LEP STRATEGY: To revise their work, pair ESL/LEP students with students fluent in English. The fluent English speakers can help the ESL/LEP students to find wording that clearly and forcefully expresses their opinions while respecting the audience's opinions. The fluent English speaker will gain a clearer understanding of the revision process by helping another student.

Lesson 2
Apply It

You may want to instruct the students to point out only the sentences or words that need correction. Allow the student whose essay is being read to figure out the correct punctuation, grammar, or spelling.

ESL/LEP STRATEGY: The same pairs of students who worked together in Lesson 1 can work together again to proofread their drafts.

Lesson 3
Apply It

You may want students to write out plans that describe the steps they will follow to get their essays to their intended audiences. Evaluate these plans according to the following criteria: (1) Is the plan too generalized? Is it so detailed that it cannot be carried out in a reasonable amount of time? (2) Are steps missing? Are unnecessary steps included? (3) Have they followed any rules or guidelines necessary for a particular method of publishing? (4) Has the essay been prepared in a form most useful to the publishing method chosen? For example, has a letter to the editor been type-written, a speech written out on index cards, or a poster drawn in an eye-catching design? (5) Have they anticipated any "roadblocks" they may have to contend with in publishing their essays? Encourage students to follow through with their plans.

WHAT HAVE YOU LEARNED IN UNIT 2?

1. You will more than likely already have ideas about facts and examples that support your opinion. You can more easily argue the case for something you feel strongly about.

2. By narrowing your topic, you can write an essay that covers the assignment in the time and space available to you. A topic that is too generalized may be hard to support with facts and reasons.

3. You want your audience to understand what you are saying. To accomplish this, you must understand the person or people to whom you are speaking.

4. Having a clear idea of what you are trying to accomplish with your essay will help you keep the essay focused and well supported with facts and arguments. You want your audience to have a clear understanding of the opinion you are presenting.

5. Your audience must understand *why* you hold your particular opinion. You need to gather facts that show that your opinion makes sense. While your audience may be able to disagree with your opinion, they cannot disagree with facts.

6. You should start your essay with a strong question or statement that draws the audience in (the hook). You must identify the topic. You also need to express your opinion. End the paragraph with your most important reason for holding that opinion.

7. The body of your essay should present facts, reasons, and examples that support the opinion stated in the introduction. Answer objections to your opinion before they can be made.

8. The conclusion should include a restatement of the opinion presented in the introductory paragraph. The audience should be urged to agree with your opinion. You can suggest that your audience take action. You should end the conclusion with a strong positive statement.

9. When you revise, you make changes to ensure that your ideas have been expressed clearly. You can improve what you have already written by cutting unnecessary words, checking that your opinions have been expressed in a strong yet moderate tone, and clarifying your wording.

10. When you proofread you look for and fix any errors in spelling, grammar, and punctuation.

UNIT NOTE:

You may want to write the "Tips for Writing Persuasive Essays" on the chalkboard or have the students make a poster of the tips that can be hung in the classroom for future reference.

UNIT 3 Writing on Your Own

Apply It

From the samples that the students have gathered, have each of them choose one example of each type of writing. Direct them to read each example carefully. Then have them look for common elements found in all three examples. Students may notice that all are written to get the audience to agree with the writer; have a central topic; have an introduction, body, and conclusion; have introductions that state the writer's position; have bodies that support the opinion with facts; have conclusions that tell what the writer thinks, urge the reader to action (sometimes), and end with a closing statement. Students will learn about the differences among the types of persuasive writing as they read the unit.

COOPERATIVE LEARNING STRATEGY: You can conduct this activity using groups. Provide each group with one sample of each type of persuasive writing. Have them write a list of common elements. Have the groups share their lists.

Chapter 1
Writing a Letter to the Editor
Review It

1. Angela states that the bike riders in the Mud Riders Club do not harm the mountains.
2. Angela states the following facts: that club members do not bike on prohibited trails; that they never leave trash in the woods; and that they always ride in a way that does not put others at risk.
3. She urges them to join or form their own bike clubs.

CHAPTER NOTES:

This chapter will require students to choose topics on which to write letters to the editor in response to articles they have read. You may want to plan for time at the library to give students access to various newspapers and magazines.

You can have the students write down ideas for responses to several articles. Then guide each student in choosing a response that will work well for this assignment. The response chosen should have at least two possible reasons for its support.

Have students write down the addresses for the editors of the magazines to which they will be writing. They will need them later in the chapter.

Lesson 1
Review It

The following facts should have check marks beside them: *Some trails wear away quickly and are not good for biking; Some trails do not wear away easily and are good for biking;* and *Most riders in my club are willing to share.*

Apply It

Students' idea branches will vary depending on the subject chosen. Each diagram should show at least two reasons for making a particular response. All reasons should be supported by at least one verifiable fact.

Lesson 2
Apply It

The introduction of a well-written plan will: (1) identify the article; (2) briefly state the idea being responded to; (3) state the writer's response; and (4) not contain superfluous information.

The body of the plan will: (1) state the reasons or facts written in the idea branch in the lesson; (2) make the point immediately; and (3) not contain any points that will require additional facts or make the letter too long.

The conclusion of the plan will: (1) tell the readers what to think; (2) urge the readers to agree and perhaps take action; and (3) end with a positive statement.

Lesson 3
Apply It

Keep in mind that the students have been told not to be concerned with grammar and spelling. Drafting a strong, direct letter is their primary goal in this lesson.

A well-written draft will follow the notes students made in Lesson 2. Use the checklist on p. 46 of the student book to evaluate whether students have properly revised and proofread their drafts.

COOPERATIVE LEARNING STRATEGY: If students are working with partners, you may want each partner to write a list of the revisions he or she believes the other partner should make. Evaluate how well the student responded to those suggestions and how helpful those suggestions were.

Chapter 2
Writing a Speech Urging Action
Review It

1. People should fight pollution and clean up Napoli creek.
2. Juan states two facts: factories dump chemicals into the creek, and water that was once clear is now cloudy.
3. Juan urges his audience to get the city government to make the factories follow clean-water laws. He also asks them to volunteer to clean up the litter in the creek.

Lesson 1
Apply It

When evaluating the idea webs, be sure that the central idea is clearly stated and well focused. Check that the reasons stated in the circle are reasonably related to the central idea.

Lesson 2
LESSON NOTES:

Review the difference between facts and opinions. Opinions are people's feelings on a subject. Opinions cannot be proved. Facts are statements that can be proved.

Apply It

A well-organized chart will: (1) contain a clear statement of the student's chosen position in the "topic" box; (2) have opinions and facts listed in the proper box; (3) list facts that can be verified; and (4) contain only opinions that are well related to the topic written at the top of the chart.

Lesson 3
Apply It

Encourage students to write down as many actions as they can think of. They can eliminate those that do not seem reasonable afterward, as shown in the example.

In deciding which actions are most easily carried out, ask the students' to think of how they would accomplish the tasks they are requesting of their audience.

Lesson 4
Apply It

Evaluate the students' speech drafts by seeing how well they followed the checklist on p. 51 of the student book.

Lesson 5
Apply It

Use the revision checklists on pages 35 and 52 of the student book to evaluate the students' speeches. Also consider the students' use of grammar, punctuation, and spelling in your evaluation. Because these speeches are meant to be read aloud, note the students' use of language in your evaluation. Check that they do not use phrases, idioms, or clichés that will sound awkward when spoken.

You may want to schedule several speeches a day, giving each student adequate time to present his or her position and lead a discussion. You might also want to arrange for some of the more powerful or relevant speeches to be presented to other classes.

COOPERATIVE LEARNING STRATEGY: When students are working with partners, have one partner read his or her speech all the way through once while the other partner takes notes on how the speech can be improved. The speech writers will feel that they've been given the opportunity to present their entire arguments before they will be asked to make changes. The partners can then go over the speech again to correct any errors and make improvements.

Chapter 3
Writing a Letter of Complaint
Review It

1. The circled words should be: *Corco portable stereo* and *model #4123.*
2. The circled words should be: *Scott's Store in Dayton, Ohio.*
3. The underlined sentence should be: *I have enclosed a copy of my sales slip.*
4. The underlined sentence should be: *I am dissatisfied with the stereo because the cassette recorder does not work.*
5. The underlined sentence should be: *Please send me a refund for the full amount I paid for my stereo or tell me how to return it for replacement.*

Lesson 1
Apply It

A well-organized chart will: (1) contain a clear statement of the student's chosen position in the "complaint" box; (2) have opinions and facts listed in the proper box; (3) list facts that can be verified; (4) contain only opinions that are well related to the topic and written in a non-offensive manner; (5) rely more on the facts than on opinions; and (6) have a forceful yet positive overall tone.

Lesson 2
LESSON NOTES:

Remind students that they can initially list the facts and opinions for the bodies of their letters in any order. They can then go back to number them in order of importance.

Apply It

Students' planning charts will vary depending on their topics. However, they should follow the

general organization described in What to Do on p. 55 of the student book.

Lesson 3
Apply It

The students' drafts of their letters of complaint can be evaluated according to how well they followed the checklist provided on p. 57 of the student book.

Lesson 4
Apply It

Use the revision checklists on pages 35 and 58 of the student book to evaluate the students' letters. Also consider the students' use of grammar, punctuation, and spelling in the evaluation.

Have students keep copies of their letters. If any of the students receive responses, have them bring their original letters and responses to class. If a response is unsatisfactory, have the student note whether any portion of the letter could have been written differently to elicit a more positive response.

WHAT HAVE YOU LEARNED IN UNIT 3?

1. You write a letter to the editor when an article you have read makes you happy or angry and you want the editor or other readers of the article to know it.
2. Topics that are best for a letter to the editor are those that can be supported by facts, examples, and reasons.
3. Make your point. Urge the readers to agree with you. You can also urge them to take a specific action. End the conclusion with a positive statement.
4. A speech urging action is intended to make others agree with your opinion on an issue and want to do something about it.
5. Begin with a salutation that identifies your audience. Follow this with a hook that leads into your opinion. State your topic. State your opinion on the topic.
6. Restate your position on the topic. Ask the audience to agree with you. Urge the

audience to take a reasonable action. End with a strong, positive statement.

7. Revise the speech, making sure that it contains all the elements of good persuasive writing and a well-written speech. Proofread it for grammar, punctuation, and spelling. Check the pronunciation of unfamiliar words or names. Read it aloud to hear how it will sound to others.

8. A letter of complaint protects your rights as a consumer. It lets a manufacturer or other business know that you are not satisfied with their product or service. It also gives that business the opportunity to correct the problem.

9. A letter of complaint should follow the basic format of a persuasive essay: an introduction, a body, and a conclusion. It should also begin with your return address, followed by the company's address. A salutation to identify and address your audience should precede the introduction. A formal close such as "Sincerely," should follow your conclusion. Your letter should be signed above your printed or typed name.

10. Your letter of complaint should identify the product or service. It should include information about where your purchase was made or service was received. Identify the type of proof of purchase or receipt of service you have included with your letter. Your complaint should be clearly stated and presented with reasons or facts backing your complaint.

UNIT NOTE:
You may want to write the tips for the three kinds of writing the students did in this unit on the board or have the students make posters of the tips that can be hung in the classroom for future reference. You can divide the class into three groups and assign one poster to each group.

UNIT 4 Writing on Assignment

Apply It
If students cannot find good examples of a persuasive writing test, provide them with copies of the well-written sample essay from the Assessment Guide on p. 11 of the TRM.

In looking at how the writers have persuaded their audiences, students may note that both the ads and the test essays use descriptive language, appeal to the senses, use facts or reasons to support opinions or sell products, and appeal to the interests of the audience. The essays attempt to persuade the audience to agree with them while the ads attempt to persuade the audience to buy a product. In addition, students may note that the ads use color or intriguing pictures, dramatic wording, and interesting headlines to influence the audience.

Chapter 1
Writing a Test Essay
Review It
1. Answers will vary but may include some of the following facts or reasons: reading exposes you to new words, helping you to increase your vocabulary; reading stimulates your mind in a way that passive viewing of television does not; reading expands your imagination by allowing you to picture yourself in the character's place; reading about different philosophies teaches you new ways to think.
2. Answers will vary.

Apply It
Students' essays will vary. However, a well-written essay will: (1) contain a clear statement of the student's position; (2) repeat some of the facts and reasons stated in question 1 or 2 of Review It; (3) show that the student can distinguish between fact and opinion; (4) use only the facts that support the student's stated position; and (5) be concise.

Lesson 1
Review It

1. The following phrases should be underlined: *summarize what it means; agree or disagree; support your point of view.*
2. Summarize the meaning of the author's statement.
3. State whether you agree or disagree with the statement.
4. Use facts and reasons to support your point of view.

Lesson 2
Review It

Students' outlines should begin with a summary of the meaning of Willa Cather's statement. Some students will interpret the statement to mean that writers' experiences as children (basic material) provide the topics or themes on which most writers write later. Others may take it to mean that the writing skills (basic material) writers acquire before the age of fifteen are the most useful skills that writers employ later on.

The next part of the outline should be a statement of the student's opinions on the topic.

The outline should be followed by a cluster diagram. The diagram should contain a number of facts and reasons that support the student's opinion. Facts or reasons may include: People are most impressionable when they are young; we learn our most important lessons in life as children; most of our education has taken place by the time we are fifteen.

Lesson 3
Apply It

Have students submit both their notes for the test essay and their drafts of the test essay. Evaluate the work based on how well they followed the steps outlined on p. 65 of the student book. Especially note how well the students meet the standards for a well-written introduction, body, and conclusion. However, save your final evaluation, using the Assessment Guide, until Lesson 4.

Lesson 4
Apply It

Use the checklist provided on p. 67 of the student book and the Assessment Guide on pp. 9-14 of the TRM to evaluate the students' essays.

Chapter 2
Writing an Advertisement
Review It

1. The product being advertised is a home-video game.
2. The product's name is *Star Challenger*.
3. The company that makes the game is Bingo Game Wizards.
4. Details given about the product include the following: You get to be the captain; you lead the expedition to Jupiter; you design the spaceship; you decide how to get the ship out of trouble; you decide which aliens to meet.
5. Students' answers will vary but may include: science fiction fans; video game players; teenagers; adults; scientists. Accept all reasonable answers.
6. Persuasive words or phrases include: *Captain, your ship awaits! Blast off to Jupiter; exciting; new; fun; most popular and most successful; proudly; space-age; once-in-a-lifetime chance; right in your own home; blockbuster.*
7. The ad tells you to ask for their video game at your video store.

Apply It

Students should collect at least five ads. Below each ad in their notebooks, have the students jot some notes about why they find each ad persuasive.

COOPERATIVE LEARNING STRATEGY: Divide the class into groups, or "advertising teams." Assign each student one of the following roles. Depending on the size of the group, you may assign more than one student to a role. The role of writer involves the most responsibility; you may want to assign two or three students for this role.

CLIENT: Decides what product is to be advertised; will be responsible for deciding who the target audience is
EXECUTIVE: Will act as team organizer; will lead the discussion of where the ad will be presented (magazines, billboards, mass transit posters, etc.)
DESIGNER: Comes up with the design of the ad
WRITER(S): Writes the ad copy
RECORDER: Records and organizes information presented at the team meetings

All members of the team should participate in the group discussions. Compromises among team members are essential for the success of the project. Their goals will be the same as those of an individual student completing this project.

Though tasks have been assigned to specific team members, all members should feel free to contribute ideas and offer suggestions for improvement for all phases of this project. For each meeting, each team member should pre-read the lesson and come prepared with any ideas or notes necessary.

Lesson 1
Apply It
Students' product profile charts should show that they've thought about and answered the questions in What to Do. The charts should also reflect that an effort has been made to match the product features to the audience's interests, wants, and needs—not the other way around.

COOPERATIVE LEARNING STRATEGY: The client will be responsible for deciding who the target audience is. The entire team should be involved in deciding the audience's interests, wants, and needs; the features that will appeal to them; and the features that make the product different or special.

Lesson 2
Apply It
Encourage all students to use a thesaurus and to refer to the ads they have collected in their notebooks for ideas on how to use descriptive words and phrases. Evaluate students on how well they are able to notice the subtle differences among words with similar meanings but different connotations.

ESL/LEP STRATEGY: Pair an ESL/LEP student with a student proficient in English. The English-proficient student can help the ESL/LEP student learn the negative and positive connotations of which the student may be unaware.

COOPERATIVE LEARNING STRATEGY: The writer or writers will be responsible for drafting the word diagrams for the product features. The entire team will then meet to discuss the positive and negative connotations of the words in the diagrams.

Lesson 3
Apply It
Use the following criteria to evaluate the drafts of the students' ads: (1) the grabber should draw the reader to the ad; (2) to draft the main text the students should pick up the information from the product profile chart from Lesson 1 and the positive word diagram from Lesson 2; (3) the design should clearly display the product and have text in a position that makes the audience read it; and (4) the text should clearly describe what the product is and why the audience needs it.

Be generous in viewing the art. Not all students have talent in that area.

COOPERATIVE LEARNING STRATEGY: The entire team should brainstorm on ideas for the "grabber." The writer or writers will be responsible for the final wording of the headline. The designer should draw sketches of several ideas for the ad including the art, the typeface for the text and headline, and how the text and art will look on the page. The team should choose the final design. The writer or writers should use the recorder's notes, the product profile chart from Lesson 1, and the positive word diagram from Lesson 2 to draft the main text.

Lesson 4
Apply It

To evaluate the quality of the students' ads, use the checklist on p. 73 of the student book.

COOPERATIVE LEARNING STRATEGY: Have one team "test market" their ad to another team. The recorder should write down the ideas and suggestions from their test audience.

Afterward, the writer(s) should revise and proofread. The rest of the team can give proofreading and revision suggestions for the final text. The designer should submit the final art and layout to the team.

WHAT HAVE YOU LEARNED IN UNIT 4?

1. A test essay prompt is a question or set of directions.
2. You should look for exactly what the prompt asks or tells you to do.
3. You can quickly organize your thoughts by making an outline of the key steps in answering the prompt and using a cluster diagram of notes on facts and reasons that support your opinion.
4. You should give yourself a few minutes to proofread your essay to make sure no important information is missing and to correct spelling, punctuation, and grammar.
5. You should use your strongest reason first so that if you run out of time, you will have at least presented your best argument to support your opinion.
6. The purpose of an advertisement is to persuade the audience to buy the product.
7. It is important to think about the audience for an ad because you will need your ad to appeal directly to those people. To do this, you must know what features of your product will interest them.
8. Connotations of words are the suggested meaning, or tone, of the words.
9. You would use words with positive connotations to give your audience a positive feeling about your product. You do not want to use words that might disinterest or perhaps even offend your audience.
10. Testing your ads gives you the opportunity to make changes to better target your audience and describe your product.

UNIT NOTE:

You might want to have students compile a list of the areas in which they had the most trouble. Have the students focus on these problems and share their solutions.

For classes that worked as advertising teams, let each team come up with a list of what worked best in their group. You might prefer to have the teams that wrote the more successful ads share their lists with the other groups.

UNIT 1 Understanding Narration

Review It

1. The purpose of narrative writing is to tell a story.
2. The following are kinds of narrative writing: a personal narrative; an eyewitness account; a humorous anecdote.
3. Any two of the following guidelines can be listed: build your story around a plot or a series of events; focus on a conflict; present interesting characters; have the action take place in a particular setting; have a narrator tell the story from a particular point of view; include a central theme.

Chapter 1
Starting with the Basics
Review It

1. The characters in the anecdote are the narrator, the narrator's grandparents, the narrator's brother (Tony), and the narrator's mother.
2. The setting is the narrator's kitchen.
3. Students' answers will vary, but may include: excited; proud; happy.
4. The grandfather didn't stop eating, which the narrator took as a compliment. Then the grandmother commented that the grandfather would eat anything.

Lesson 1
Review It

The students may take a number of different approaches to rewriting the beginning of Jasmine's narrative. To begin with a detail of a character, students may cut the first few sentences and go right into the description of Raymond and Henry as avid baseball fans. To begin with a detail of the plot, they might write about how Raymond, Henry, and the narrator all watched baseball together. To begin with a

detail of the setting, students might describe the room in which everyone watched the ball game or how it felt to be in the room with Raymond and the uncle.

To begin with a dialogue, students might open with a brief conversation between Raymond and Uncle Henry about baseball or between the narrator and Raymond or Uncle Henry.

To hint where the narrative might lead, students might write a sentence or two about a particular time they watched a ball game together, without giving too many details yet.

Lesson 2
Review It

1. They are devoted fans of opposing baseball teams.
2. The outcome of a player's last chance at bat will decide whether the game goes into extra innings. Also, the player at bat has been in a slump all season. These two situations increase the tension between the two friends.

Lesson 3
Review It

1. The strategies that should be underlined are: *end with a thought that will stay in your readers' minds; end with a quotation; solve the conflict.*
2. The batter hits a home run.
3. Seeing the player hit a home run makes everyone happy.

Chapter 2
Narrating with Style
Apply It

One major difference students may notice in narrative styles is the point of view. Some may be written in the first person while others are in the third person. Ask them to think about how the differences in the narrator's point of view influences the feel of the writing examples. Other differences they may notice are the use of or lack of dialogue, the scope of the topic (narrow or broad), the presence of a plot as opposed to a sequence of related events, and the manner of opening (a statement of facts, the introduction of a character, a description of the setting).

Lesson 1
Review It
1. Sense-of-sight details include the phrases: *so wet they stuck to our skin; sprouted from the ground like a mushroom; dark as a cave; gleamed; sparkled like polished trophies.*
2. The one sense-of-smell detail is: *smelled like a giant sweat sock.*
3. Students' replies may include sense-of-hearing details that refer to the way sound traveled through the arena, the sounds of the basketball bouncing, the sounds of the players moving, speaking, whispering, or shouting, and so on.

ESL/LEP STRATEGY:
Encourage ESL/LEP students to expand their use of descriptive expression in English. Review the use of *like* or *as if* as tools to more descriptive language. For example, instead of *quiet* or *red*, use *so quiet it was as if we were wearing ear plugs*, or *red as a ripe, shiny apple*. Write some non-descript adjectives (such as blue, loud, sweet, and lumpy) on the board. Then have the students write a descriptive phrase using each adjective.

Lesson 2
Review It
1. The following pronouns should be underlined: *I* (three times); *my* (twice).
2. Students sentences should relate to the paragraph and use the pronouns *I, me,* or *we.*
3. The rewritten first sentence should be similar to: *Jose and his sister Maya leaned their elbows on the ledge of the window.*

ESL/LEP STRATEGY:
To reinforce the ESL/LEP students' understanding of the proper use of pronouns, have them review the Pronouns section of the *Guide for Writers: Grammar, Mechanics, and Usage* on p. 76 of the student book.

Lesson 3
Review It
1. He rides the bus to the concert hall.
2. All the fans were dancing in the aisles.
3. Transitional words and phrases should include: *early that evening; at first; after a while; soon.*

WHAT HAVE YOU LEARNED IN UNIT 1?
1. Narrative writing is writing that tells a story
2. There are three kinds of conflict the student may use. The conflict can be a struggle between two characters. It can be a struggle between a character and nature. It can be a struggle within a character.
3. Sensory details should be included. Sensory details tell what can be seen, heard, felt, tasted, or smelled.
4. The plot is the sequence of events that shapes the story. It helps the reader make sense of the events. A weak plot will make a story hard to follow.
5. The theme explains the importance of the events being described. Having a central message often makes the narrative more interesting.
6. There are four strategies for beginning a narrative. Begin with an introduction of the narrative's most interesting character. Begin with a detail of a character, the plot, or the setting. Begin with a dialogue. Begin with a hint of where the narrative might lead.
7. There are seven strategies for ending a narrative. End with a thought that will stay in your reader's mind. End with a quotation. End the suspense. Solve the conflict. Tell about the importance of the event. Tell what a character learned from the event. Tell what happens to a character years later.
8. Sensory details more vividly describe the characters and setting. They help the readers imagine the feelings of a character or imagine that they are at the scene of the narrative themselves.

9. You should use the first-person point of view for a personal narrative.
10. The use of transitions establishes the chronological order of the events of the plot.

UNIT NOTE:

Write the words "Five Great Ways to Tell a Story" on the board or have the students make a poster of the tips that can be hung in the classroom for future reference.

UNIT 2 Writing To Tell a Story

Apply It

If you choose to have students work individually, have them write down their thoughts as they imagine each step. To help the students focus on the planning stage of writing a story, ask them to think about such questions as: How would they decide on the topic? Who do they think the intended audience is? Why would they write about such a topic? Where would they gather information to use in their writing?

COOPERATIVE LEARNING STRATEGY:

Divide the class into groups. Provide each group with an example of a short story from a magazine and a brief lesson from a history book. Ask the groups to make lists of the differences between the two styles of narrative writing.

Students may notice such differences as: the narrative of the history lesson is strictly chronological while the short story may jump around in time; the history lesson uses fewer or no sensory details while the short story does; the kinds of conflicts may be different; and so on.

Have the groups read their lists aloud to compare. Write a master list on the board of all the differences the groups found. Then ask them to think about why the different styles were used. Answers should focus on the difference in what each writing sample was trying to convey (facts vs. a story).

Chapter 1
Planning Your Writing
Apply It
Remind students at the end of each lesson to return to this list.

Lesson 1
LESSON NOTE:
Remind students to use only events that actually occurred and which they, themselves, have experienced.

Apply It

Answers to questions 1-4 are based solely on the students' personal opinions. There are no right or wrong answers. However, you may want to offer some guidance on the final choice of topics made by the students. Remind the students to keep the topic general. They will have a chance to narrow its focus in Lesson 2.

Lesson 2
Apply It

Topic webs will vary depending on how narrow or broad the original topics were. However, a well thought out web will contain at least two "spin-off" ideas.

Lesson 3
Apply It

Answer to questions 1 and 2 will vary depending on the topic chosen. A good answer to question 2 will show a clear understanding of the audience chosen. Check whether the students have clearly identified what information will be necessary to tell an interesting story.

Lesson 4
Review It

1. Some feelings students may express are frightened, in suspense, tense, confused, intrigued, or curious.
2. Details used to create the feeling of tension are: how the wind became so cold that he shivered; how the wind grew stronger until the treetops swayed; how the sky became dark; how the thunder crashed; how everything was suddenly quiet.

Apply It

Students' sentences should in some way refer to a feeling or emotion they'd like to evoke in their audience.

Lesson 5
Apply It

Students should have at least one answer for each of the questions of *who, what, when, where,* *why,* and *how.* They should also have at least one sensory detail for each of the senses. At this stage, students need not use descriptive phrases (beginning with *like* and *as if*) in noting the sensory details. For example, *salty* and *dark* are sufficient.

Lesson 6
Apply It

The topic should be the central idea from their topic web in Lesson 2. The central idea should be the focused topic from that same web. The events should be listed in the order in which they occurred. The students will have to decide at which point they want to end their stories. This final event should be written in the conclusion box.

Lesson 7
Apply It

Use the checklist from the What to Do section on p. 27 of the student book to evaluate how well the students have met the criteria for each element (conflict, rising action, climax, and resolution) of a well thought out plot.

Chapter 2
Developing Your Writing
Apply It

Remind students at the end of each lesson to return to this list.

Lesson 1
Review It

1. Students should underline the sentence: *Dark clouds rumbled across the sky.*
2. Actions that can be underlined are: *shooting; jumped; whipped; shivered; rumbled.*
3. Students' answers will vary but may include: sweltering, steaming, scorching, boiling.

Apply It

Evaluate the strength of the students' opening paragraphs using the following criteria: (1) How well did they transfer the ideas from their event maps (student book p. 26) or plot profiles (student book p. 28) and sensory detail webs (student book p. 24)? (2) How well would their opening sentences grab the readers' attention? (3) How well did they integrate the key elements (setting the scene, introducing character, establishing the conflict)?

Lesson 2
Review It

1. If the students take the question literally, they will reply that raindrops fell on Jamal's face. A more general answer would state that while Jamal continued to play basketball, he saw the sky change.

2. The literal answer would be that Jamal continued to play ball. The more general answer would be that the weather changed dramatically.

3. The words or phrases that should be underlined are: *suddenly; then; all at once; suddenly.*

Apply It
Evaluate the strength of the middle sections of the students' essays using the following criteria: (1) How well did they transfer the ideas from their event maps (student book p. 26) or plot profiles (student book p. 28) and sensory detail webs (student book p. 24)? (2) How well did they describe what action was taking place and why it was happening? (3) How well did they establish the chronology of the events and use transitional words and phrases?

Lesson 3
Review It

1. The conflict is resolved when the tornado moves on.

2. The suspense ends when Jamal hears the birds chirping, and he stands up.

Apply It
Evaluate the strength of the students' conclusions to their essays using the following criteria: (1) How well did they transfer the ideas from their event maps (student book p. 26) or plot profiles (student book p. 28) and sensory detail webs

(student book p. 24)? (2) Did they successfully employ any of the manners of closing listed on p. 32 of the student book? (3) Does the conclusion provide a satisfying close to their story?

Chapter 3
Completing Your Writing
Apply It
Remind students at the end of each lesson to return to this list.

Lesson 1
Apply It
Evaluation of the students' work in this lesson should be based on how well they followed the steps outlined in the checklist on p. 35 of the student book and on how much of an improvement they made from the original draft. Few students are able to write their best essay in one draft.

ESL/LEP STRATEGY: Pair a proficient English-speaker with a less proficient one. Have the more proficient student give the other student specific help with English phrasing or idioms and with expanding the student's descriptive vocabulary.

Lesson 2
Apply It
Remind students to concentrate on proof-reading. This is not the time for rewriting. The rewriting stage of this assignment should have been completed in Lesson 1 of this chapter. Students' essays should be evaluated only for grammar, spelling, and punctuation.

Lesson 3
Review It
Students' opinions on their favorites will vary.

COOPERATIVE LEARNING STRATEGY:
Divide the class into groups according to the title they preferred. Have the groups confer separately on the reasons why they chose the titles they did. Then engage the groups in a discussion of the merits and weaknesses of each title.

Apply It

Students can write plans that describe the steps they will follow to have their essays published. Encourage students to follow through with their plans.

WHAT HAVE YOU LEARNED IN UNIT 2?

1. Students' answers should vary and should not be the same as the title for the essay they have already written in this unit.

2. Answers will vary but may include that the topic: is important to them (preferably they will explain *why* the topic is important to them); is interesting; will make their audiences think; is funny or entertaining.

3. The two kinds of details needed in a narrative are details about the event and sensory details that help the readers experience the event.

4. The beginning of a narrative essay should: include an opening sentence that lures in the reader; set the scene; introduce the most importance characters; establish a conflict.

5. The middle of the essay should describe the events or plot of your story. It's where the action takes place.

6. The end of the narrative essay should contain the resolution of the plot. The essay can end in the following ways: with a thought that will stay in the readers' minds; with a quotation; by ending the suspense; by resolving the conflict and tying up loose ends; by explaining the importance of the events to the characters in the story; by telling what a character learned; by telling what happened to a character later on.

7. When you revise, you strengthen and improve your writing to ensure that you've told your story clearly.

8. When you proofread, you fix any mistakes in spelling, punctuation, and grammar.

9. Students' answers will vary depending on their experience with this project.

10. All students, regardless of how well they completed their essays, should be able to find ways to make their writing go more smoothly next time.

UNIT NOTE:

Have each group choose one member to represent them. Then have the representatives discuss their groups' lists. Ask them to come up with a master list of "Tips for Writing Narrative Essays" and reproduce it as a pamphlet for use by the rest of the class.

UNIT3 Writing On Your Own

Review It

From the samples that the students have gathered, have each of them choose one example of each type of writing. Direct them to read each example carefully. Then have them look for common elements found in all three examples. Students may notice that all tell a story; have a central topic; have an introductory paragraph that describes the setting, introduces characters, and gets the action started; have a middle that tells the events of the story; and may be told in chronological order (personal narratives may be the exception). Note the ways in which the endings of the three examples differ significantly. Students will learn about other differences as they read the unit.

COOPERATIVE LEARNING STRATEGY:

You can conduct this activity using groups. Provide each group with one sample of each type of narrative writing. Have each group brainstorm a list of common elements. Have the groups share their lists.

Chapter 1
Writing a Personal Narrative
Review It

1. The names that should be underlined are *Maria* and *New Shoes*.
2. The details used to describe Maria are: *a girl, long braids and red ribbons; smiled.*
3. The sentence that tells where the narrative takes place is: *I stood against the scratchy brick wall, watching the other kids play basketball.*
4. Maria befriended Rosa when she was a lonely new student at school. Maria, having been a new student the year before, is able to empathize with how Rosa felt.

Lesson 1
LESSON NOTE:

Remind students to use only events that actually occurred and which they, themselves, have experienced.

Apply It

Students should be encouraged to think of at least three events for each limb of the idea branch. Guide students in choosing the events that they will use for the rest of this chapter. Ask them to be sure that the event each of them chooses is a topic they will feel comfortable sharing with the rest of the class.

Lesson 2
Apply It

Students should have at least one answer to each of the questions *who, what, where, when, why,* and *how.* They should also have at least one sensory detail for each of the senses. At this point in the chapter, the answers to the questions and the sensory details need only supply the basic information.

Lesson 3
Review It

1. The pronouns that should be underlined are: *I* (six times) and *my.*
2. The pronouns that should be underlined are: *She* (twice), *her* (six times).
3. While Rosa felt badly that Maria was ill and missed her, Rosa's visits to Maria made her feel better.

Apply It

Students' additions to their notes should reflect a clear understanding of the first-person point of view. Their notes should express their views and feelings rather than that of any other character in their narrative. Students may want to add another "layer" of circles to their sensory detail diagrams describing their feelings about those details.

Lesson 4
Review It
Accept any changes that students make that simplify, clarify, improve the story's flow, or add interest.

Apply It
Students should submit both their drafts and final essays. The essays should show improvement between the draft and final version. To evaluate the final version, see how well the student has followed the revision and proofreading checklists provided on p. 46 of the student book. Also check the essays for grammar, spelling, and punctuation.

After the students have produced clean copies of their final essays, you can have the essays assembled into an anthology. The anthology can be photocopied and distributed to the class.

Chapter 2
Writing an Eyewitness Account
Review It
1. The sentence that should be underlined is: *When we arrived on the scene, firefighters were aiming gigantic water hoses at the upper floors.*
2. The two sentences that give details are: *Flames shot from the roof of the apartment building. A strong wind fed the fire.*
3. The sentence that shows the importance of the event is: *The people on the sidewalk, now homeless, would be able to read all about it in the morning paper.*

Lesson 1
Review It
If students are having trouble understanding the assignment, ask them questions such as the following to guide them: What doors flew open? What color were the doors? What kind of athlete is seen? What did the athlete look like? How many fans were there? What were the fans like? What kind of smile? Is there a more descriptive word to use rather than *smile*? What word can you use in place of *traveled*? How far

or for how long did the narrator travel?
Also remind students to use sensory details whenever possible.

Apply It
Students may first want to write out the general events of their topics. Then, just as they did in Review It, they may go back to add more vivid details.

Lesson 2
Review It
The underlined words and phrases should be: *When we arrived at the scene; as soon as he was out of the car; then.*

Apply It
Students' chains of events will depend on the story they are telling. Be sure that the events are listed chronologically. Each event should have details listed under *Notes* that will help the student write a clear and interesting eyewitness account.

Lesson 3
Apply It
The draft of the eyewitness account can be evaluated by how well the student followed the guidelines on p. 51 of the student book.

Lesson 4
Apply It
Evaluate the accounts by how well the students followed the revision checklist on p. 35 of the student book and how well they have integrated the key elements of an eyewitness account listed on p. 52 of the student book. Also evaluate how well they followed through with publishing their accounts.

Chapter 3
Drafting a Humorous Anecdote
Review It
1. The names that should be circle are *Jesse (I), Franklin* and *Uncle Eli.*
2. The examples of dialogue are: *I said, "It's*

strength, not length.”; My brother yelled, “You’re wrong! Big-league pitchers have longer arms than normal people.”; and Uncle Eli answered, “Well, I think a big-league pitcher needs a throwing arm that reaches all the way from his shoulder to his hand.”

3. Uncle Eli reveals that he is a moderator; he chooses not to take sides. He also displays his sense of humor.

Lesson 1
Review It
1. A humorous anecdote builds to a punch line.
2. He and his brother disagree about the length of a pitcher’s arm.
3. Students’ answers will vary but some might suggest that the argument was silly to begin with, that the answer didn’t really matter, or that Uncle Eli gave a funny answer in a serious manner.

Apply It
Have students write ideas for their anecdotes on separate sheets of paper. They may want to jot down brief paragraphs summarizing the story. Then have them move on to the event map. Remind them that they do not have to think of the exact wording of the events or punch line for this lesson.

Lesson 2
Apply It
Students may include details on the people, dialogue, the point of the anecdote, and the actual punch line. Students should be able to think of at least one detail for each event.

Lesson 3
Apply It
Use the checklist on p. 58 of the student book to evaluate how well the student has met the criteria for a well-written draft.

Students should have kept in mind that the anecdote must be brief. Students will have an opportunity for cutting in the next lesson.

Lesson 4
Apply It
You may want to ask students to identify what details make their anecdotes funny. Students’ anecdotes can be evaluated using the checklist on pages 35 and 59 of the student book. Also evaluate grammar, spelling, and punctuation.

ESL/LEP STRATEGY: Because of differences in language and the nature of humor, ESL students may not understand the humor of certain anecdotes. Have them write down the titles of any anecdotes they do not understand. The writers of the anecdotes can then explain what made their stories funny.

WHAT HAVE YOU LEARNED IN UNIT 3?
1. In a personal narrative, the narrator is telling a story about himself or herself.
2. You can gather details for your narrative by asking yourself *who, what, where,when, why,* and *how* questions. You can also make a sensory details web.
3. In the conclusion of a personal narrative, you should bring your story to a clear ending.
4. In an eyewitness account, you tell a story about a first-hand experience.
5. A vivid detail is specific, appeals to at least one of the five senses, and provides a complete description.
6. The purpose of a chain of events chart is to provide a clear progression of your story in the order in which it occurred.
7. The ending of an eyewitness account should explain the importance of the event (what it meant to you or others).
8. Important characteristic of a humorous anecdote are that it is: brief, entertains the reader, is often about real people, usually uses dialogue, and may make a point or reveal a personality trait.
9. An anecdote can be funny because it: exaggerates wildly, gives an unexpected twist, includes unexpected details about a setting or character, or tells about a ridiculous situation in a serious tone.

10. The very last element of a humorous anecdote should be the punch line.

UNIT NOTE:

Students may have had particular trouble with the brevity of a humorous anecdote. Have students go over their stories within small groups of four students and give one another ideas about which details are unnecessary and can be cut. They can ask questions such as: Does this help build to my punch line or does it steer away from my point? Will the humor be understood without this detail? How can I combine ideas?

UNIT 4 Writing On Assignment

Apply It

If students cannot find good examples of a narrative writing test, provide them with copies of the well-written sample essay from the Assessment Guide on p. 16 of the TRM.

Students may notice that, in general, the biographies follow a basic pattern. They open with an introduction of the subject of the biography. The biographies go on to tell the story of the subject's life. Along the way, the importance of this person—either to society, the narrator, or reader—is revealed.

By comparing their examples, students may see that test essays also follow a certain pattern. They open with a statement of the goal of the essay. The middle tells the events of the story. The conclusion sums up the intent of the essay.

Chapter 1
Writing a Test Essay
Review It

1. The first event mentioned is the gathering in Philadelphia of 55 men from 12 states.
2. It took place in the summer of 1787.
3. The underlined word should be *First*.
4. The event is the disagreement of the Virginia Plan supporters and the New Jersey Plan supporters.
5. The event is the agreement of the delegates on the Connecticut Compromise.
6. The event is the completion of the Constitution.

Lesson 1
Apply It

The key words and phrases that should be underlined are: *Trace the history of the bus boycott; Include key figures; Begin; Rosa Parks's refusal; Finish; desegregation of buses.*

Lesson 2
Apply It

If the first prompt is used, the first event on the chart should be Rosa Parks's refusal to give up her bus seat. Students can mention details such as why Rosa Parks refused to give up her seat, what happened to her after her refusal, and so on. The last event should be the desegregation of the buses. Details can include how the desegregation law was passed, how the law was implemented, and so on. Other events and details should be described in the same way. The events should be presented chronologically.

For the second test essay, the first event should be the student's first day in school. Details can include what the student was feeling that day, what he or she did, what was most memorable, and so on. The last event should be an outstanding event of the present school year. Details can include how the event made the student feel, why the event occurred, when and where it occurred, and so on. Once again, the events should be presented chronologically.

Lesson 3
Apply It

You may want to give students a set time during class to complete their test essays. Allow them to use the checklist on p. 67 of the student book. Call out the time periods noted in Apply It on p. 67 of the student book.

COOPERATIVE LEARNING STRATEGY:

For those students who had trouble completing the sample test in the time given, have them write down the problems they ran into as they tried to complete their essays. Were there several students who became stuck at the same points or with certain aspects of the writing process? Have those students work as a group with one or more proficient students on ways to tackle the problem areas of their essays.

Lesson 4
Apply It

Evaluate students' essays on: (1) how well the students answered the prompt; (2) whether important events are missing or out of order; (3) the use of transitions to smooth the flow; (4) the use of correct grammar, punctuation, and spelling; (5) how well they followed the guidelines for a well-written introduction, body, and conclusion given on p. 67 of the student book; (6) how well students were able to distinguish which errors to correct first.

Chapter 2
Writing a Biographical Account
Apply It

Encourage students to choose people whose lives will make interesting stories rather than the most convenient people who will agree to be interviewed. Have them make short lists of what they find so interesting about the people they choose.

Lesson 1
Review It

The questions that should be underlined are: *When did you come to the United States? When did that happen? When did you begin the rooftop garden?*

Apply It

Have students submit brief descriptions of their subjects and their lists of questions to you beforehand. Evaluate how well students' questions will meet their goals in interviewing their individual subjects. Check that their questions will be asked in a logical order. Also note whether the questions will help them establish a sequence of events.

COOPERATIVE LEARNING STRATEGY:

Students can work with partners to practice their interviews. The students can ask each other their questions. They can give each other feedback on how well the questions will elicit the responses needed to complete an interesting biography. They can discover if they will miss important events or not understand the proper sequence of events because of gaps in their questioning. They can also practice taking notes while the other person is speaking.

Lesson 2
Review It
The words and phrases that should be underlined are: *gets up at 5:30; after eating breakfast; before lunch; after lunch; until dinnertime.*

Apply It
Have the students write down the methods they choose for their organization. Evaluate how well they followed their plans for their writing. Each event should have at least one corresponding detail. The more details of each event that the student is able to provide, the better the essay he or she will be able to produce later on.

Lesson 3
LESSON NOTE:
This lesson includes the writing of the draft and the final version of the biography. Have students submit both their drafts and final versions. You may want to refer students to helpful checklists from earlier in the book such as writing a draft—p. 29 of the student book, revising your draft—p. 35 of the student book, and the proofreading checklists—p. 36 of the student book.

Apply It
The draft should follow the hints given on p. 73 of the student book. Evaluation of the students' drafts should be based on how well they completed the steps of writing a draft explained on p. 29 of the student book. The final biographies should show improvement from the draft. To evaluate the final version, see how well the student has followed the revision on p. 35 of the student book and proofreading checklists on p. 36 of the student book. Also check the essays for grammar, spelling, and punctuation.

After the students have produced clean copies of their final biographies, you can have them assembled into an anthology. The anthology can be photocopied and distributed to the class.

WHAT HAVE YOU LEARNED IN UNIT 4?
1. A test essay prompt is a question or set of directions.
2. You should look for exactly what the prompt asks or tells you to do.
3. You can quickly organize your thoughts by writing an outline to help put the events in order and then add brief notes on each event.
4. You should give yourself a few minutes to proofread your essay to make sure no important information is missing and to correct spelling, punctuation, and grammar.
5. Skipping lines in your draft gives you space to make changes in the revision stage of the writing process.
6. The purposes of a biographical account are: to tell the story of a real person's life or of an event in that person's life; to express your feelings about a person; to describe a person's personality; to tell how you learned something from that person.
7. The middle of a biographical account should tell the subject's story in chronological order.
8. Hints for planning an interview include: Keep your purpose in mind; Avoid "yes and no" questions; start questions with *who, what, why, when, where,* and *how;* list your questions in logical sequence; ask questions to help put events in sequence; leave space in your notes to add the answers.
9. Biographical accounts can be organized in one of the following ways: Important Events; Typical Day; Personality Traits; Road to Discovery.
10. Students' answers will vary but their answers should present a logical reason for their choice of organization.

UNIT NOTE:
Students may want to make separate lists for the different parts of writing a biographical account. One list can be "How to Conduct an Interview." Another can be "What is the Best Way to Organize this Biographical Account?" The third list can be "Writing the Biographical Account."

Notes and Answers: Writing to Explain

UNIT 1 Understanding Exposition

Apply It

You may want to go over the topics selected by the students and guide them in selecting one topic each with which they can work successfully beginning in Unit 2. Each student will need to write several ideas about the topic, then narrow its focus; identify the audience for whom he or she will be writing and the goal of the writing; and gather information and details to explain the topic.

Chapter 1
Building an Explanation
Review It

1. The three main parts of an expository essay are the introduction, the body, and the conclusion.
2. The goals of an expository essay are: (1) support your thesis or develop your main idea; (2) fit your style to your purpose; and (3) organize your material logically.

Lesson 1
Review It

1. Students' answers will vary. Some may feel that the use of this quotation grabs the attention of a reader because (1) it lets them hear someone's personal feelings; (2) it gives a first-hand account; or (3) it makes you want to hear more. Others may feel that the quotation does not grab their attention because: (1) it wasn't interesting enough; (2) they were confused about what the quoted remark referred to; or (3) the quote was too long.
2. Students may suggest one of the following strategies: (1) tell an anecdote; (2) ask a question; (3) give a startling or surprising fact; or (4) state an opinion about the topic.

Lesson 2
Review It

1. *If people would stop and think, they would recognize that they use math skills all the time.*
2. Students should realize that the next logical step in the essay is to give more examples of how math is used in their every day lives.
3. Students' answers will vary, but should indicate that once a thesis has been stated, the rest of the essay should contain examples to support that thesis.

Lesson 3
Review It

1. a cause-and-effect essay
2. a comparison-contrast essay
3. a research report
4. a summary

Lesson 4
Review It

1. Subject by Subject
2. Point by Point is another method that would have worked, though probably not as well as the method chosen. Karla could have mentioned similar details about each kind of simple machine, then explained another kind of detail, and so on. This method may have been more confusing than Subject by Subject. Chronological Order and Main Idea and Detail are organizations that would not apply to this subject. Order of Importance would also not be a choice because all the items to be discussed are of equal importance.
3. Karla will probably write about the wheel and axle next.
4. In Karla's list of all the simple machines, she mentions the lever first, then the wheel and axle. Since she writes first about the lever, she will probably follow with an explanation of the wheel and axle because it is next on the list.

Apply It

1. A compare-and-contrast essay can be organized point by point. This allows each similarity or difference between the characters to be covered together in a paragraph. A compare-and-contrast essay can also be organized subject by subject. This allows the details of one story to be completely covered before the details of the other story are discussed.

2. The purpose of the essay described is to show cause and effect. Therefore, it would be organized best in chronological order so that events of last year and this year can be clearly described and the differences explained in the order in which they happened.

3. The organization used to define a term or idea is the main idea followed by details. The main idea, the definition of *photosynthesis,* can be given and then explained with details of how it occurs.

4. The intent of the essay is to help readers see how important an idea is. Thus the essay should be organized by order of importance. The writer can begin a presentation of the argument for saving the earth's water with one reason and build toward the strongest reason.

Lesson 5
Review It

1. Paul restated his main idea.

2. Paul could have summarized the main points of his essay.

3. Student answers will vary. Since students may not be familiar with the poems, they may choose to: give readers a new idea to think about or ask a question about the main idea or thesis.

COOPERATIVE LEARNING STRATEGY: You may want to pair students for this question and assign it as extra credit. You can extend the activity by having students read the two poems before they rewrite the conclusion.

Chapter 2
Explaining with Style
Apply It

Students can use some of the samples of expository writing that they collected earlier in the unit. You may want the students to underline the transitions in the articles to see if they understand what transitions are and how they are used. You can also have them circle words and phrases that show how details make the article more interesting.

Lesson 1
Review It

1. The transitional words and phrases are: *The first thing to do, Second,* and *Therefore.*

2. Students may suggest a number of the following transitions:

To show time order: following, meanwhile, while, after a while, at the same time, soon, as soon as, finally, first (second, third, etc.), next, in the end.

To show order of importance: better, most/least important, most/least of all, equally, equal to.

To show how things are alike and different: similarly, similar to, same as, just as, differently, different from, in contrast, in the same way, on the other hand, both, neither, either, equally, equal to.

To show cause and effect: if/then, thus, hence, for that reason, due to, since, consequently, cause, make, create, determines.

To add information: as well as, in other words.

To give an example: in other words, namely, as, as follows.

Apply It

Students may write these or similar sentences using transitions. The transitions are bracketed.

1. Only two people registered for the class. [Therefore,] [As a result,] the class was canceled.

2. [In 1910,] Glacier National Park was

established in Montana.

3. Jason decided to go hiking[, though] [. However,] he had never been hiking before. [So,] [For that reason,] he sent away for literature. [He then planned] [Thus he was able to plan] [Therefore, he could plan] [Consequently, he could plan] his trip carefully.

Lesson 2
Review It

1. *Mrs. Wang is a practical, strong, caring, independent, and unselfish woman.*

2. Dan uses the anecdote of Mrs. Wang's decision regarding her husband's ability to get out of purgatory. Dan also uses a quote from Mrs. Wang that delivers the punch line of the anecdote while making her independence and strength obvious to the reader.

WHAT HAVE YOU LEARNED IN UNIT 1?

1. Using simple language, students should state that an expository essay explains something or informs someone about a subject. An expository essay tries to make a reader understand something that is difficult, unclear, or unfamiliar.

2. The purpose of the introduction is to grab the readers' attention, to make the topic and the purpose for writing clear, and to state the thesis or main idea.

3. The body of the essay is important because it supports your thesis or develops your main idea.

4. The conclusion is necessary to pull all your main points together in one paragraph and make the readers think more about your topic.

5. By stating your thesis in the introduction, the readers know the point of the essay they are about to read.

6. Knowing what you want to accomplish with your essay helps you decide the best way to explain it to your audience.

7. Organizing your essay helps you to write

clearly, make your point, and strongly support your thesis.

8. Details support your ideas, show how ideas are linked, provide examples, and show steps in a process.

9. To help your readers make connections between ideas, you should use transitions.

10. Strategies for concluding an expository essay are: summarizing the main points; restating your main idea or thesis; giving readers a new idea to think about; predicting something; asking a question about your main idea or thesis; telling a brief story to illustrate your main idea or thesis.

UNIT NOTE:

Have the students discuss their answers to the questions. Each group can make its own list of tips. Then have each group choose a representative and have the representatives get together to compile a master list. They can then present the list to the rest of the class.

UNIT 2 Writing to Explain

Apply It
If the students are working individually, have them write down their thoughts as they imagine each step. To help the students focus on the planning stage of writing exposition, ask them to think about such questions as: How would they decide on the topic? Who do they think the intended audience is? What is their purpose in writing this essay? What details will they use in their writing? How might they organize their information?

Chapter 1
Planning Your Writing
Apply It
Remind students at the end of each lesson to return to this list.

Lesson 1
LESSON NOTE:
Be sure that students have properly paired the items in the chart.

Review It
1. Students' choices will vary depending on their interests.
2. Answers will vary depending on the pair chosen by each student. Students' answers should show that they have thought about their choices and expect to learn something reasonably related to their topic.

Lesson 2
Review It
Student answers will vary, but should include at least two other sports connecting out from the broad topic: *Sports.*

Apply It
Students can use one of the topics from Lesson 1 of this chapter or they can use one of the topics they listed in Apply It of the Unit 1 opener. A well thought out web will contain at least two narrower topics connecting out from the broad topic.

Lesson 3
Review It
1. Students' most likely response will be: teenagers who ride bikes or skate.
2. The underlined phrase should be: *you guys, zipping around on skates or bikes.*

Apply It
Students can use the Audience Profile Chart on p. 103 of the TRM. They should fill in an answer for every row of the chart.

Lesson 4
Review It
1. The underlined phrase should be: *Explain how to do something.*
2. The underlined phrases should be: *safety equipment can make them fun and safe; first and most important piece of equipment.*

Apply It
Students should choose one of the purposes listed in What to Do on p. 24 of the student book.

Lesson 5
Apply It
Students' research questions should reflect that they are aware of the kinds of information they will need to explain their particular topics. Their lists of sources should be varied and show some initiative in finding unique or creative sources of information. The list should include more than just an encyclopedia, the usual source of many essays.

Lesson 6
Review It
The items that should be in the intersecting portion of the Venn diagram are helmets, good brakes and, perhaps, well-fitted and well-made equipment.

Apply It

You may want to give students blank graphic organizers to use from pp. 104–106 of the TRM. The chart on p. 26 of the student book matches the type of graphic organizer with the purpose of the essay. Students' choices of graphic organizers should match the purpose each student decided on in Lesson 4.

Chapter 2
Developing Your Writing
Apply It

Remind students at the end of each lesson to return to this list.

Lesson 1
Apply It

Students' theses should reflect the choices of narrowed topics they made in Apply It of Lesson 2 on p. 22 of the student book.

The first sentence of the introduction should draw in the reader, perhaps using one of the following methods: quote someone, tell an anecdote, ask a question, give a startling or surprising fact, or state an opinion about the topic. The thesis statement should make the point of the student's essay clear. By reading the introduction, you should be able to tell what the purpose of the essay will be.

Lesson 2
Review It

The underlined words and phrases should be: *Both; and; especially; Most; because; On the other hand; as.*

Apply It

1. After reading the students' lists, you should be able to tell how well the information to be included will support the proposed theses.
2. Students should choose words from the correct column for the type of essay they have chosen to write.
3. Aside from using transitions well, the drafts of the essay bodies should contain vivid details that enhance the clarity and interest of

the essay. They should also be well organized in a manner that suits the purpose of the essay. See p. 10 of the student book for manners of organization. The body should also contain the information the student proposed to gather on p. 25 of the student book. However, in evaluating students' work, keep in mind that these are drafts. The students will have the opportunity to improve their essays in Chapter 3 of this unit.

Lesson 3
Review It

The point of Daryl's essay is that more skaters than bicyclists use safety equipment.

Apply It

Each student's conclusion should summarize the information presented in the body of the essay. The thesis should be restated. The readers should be reminded how the thesis was supported. It should end with a final comment that grabs the readers' attention. A well-written essay will have followed most of the hints listed on p. 32 of the student book.

Chapter 3
Completing Your Essay
Apply It

Remind students at the end of each lesson to return to this list.

Lesson 1
Apply It

Students' additional questions will vary, as they should reflect their individual weaknesses in writing. Evaluate their final drafts according to how well they have improved on their drafts and how well they have executed the steps outlined in the revision checklist on p. 35 of the student book.

COOPERATIVE LEARNING STRATEGY: You may want to assign partners, pairing students of different writing abilities.

ESL/LEP STRATEGY: Pair an English-proficient student with an ESL/LEP student to review the ESL/LEP student's work. Have the English-proficient student's work reviewed by another English-proficient student.

Lesson 2
Apply It
Students' proofreading should reflect the use of the checklist and chart of proofreading symbols on p. 36 of the student book.

ESL/LEP STRATEGY: The same pairs of students who worked together in Lesson 1 can work together again to proofread the ESL/LEP students' drafts. It may be a helpful learning opportunity for the ESL/LEP students to proofread the essays written by English-proficient students also.

Lesson 3
Apply It
1. Students' choices of publishing should be a reasonable way to reach the audience they chose on p. 23 of the student book.
2. Encourage students to find and use ways to publish other than those listed. Students may want to write a plan that describes the steps they will follow to have their essays published. Encourage students to follow through with their plans.

WHAT HAVE YOU LEARNED IN UNIT 2?
1. Students' topics should be narrow enough to be covered in an essay no longer than three to five paragraphs.
2. The student should mention that: the topic should be narrow; there should be enough information available to explain it well in a few paragraphs; they should be interested in the topic.

3. You need any information that will help you explain your topic to your intended audience.
4. You need to include a thesis statement in the introduction.
5. In the body of an expository essay, you should give facts, reasons, and examples that support the thesis statement.
6. The conclusion of your essay should: include a restatement of the thesis, summarize your essay, and end with a sentence that your audience will remember.
7. To revise, you must read your draft carefully. You can then go back and make changes that ensure that you are explaining your topic and supporting your thesis exactly as you intended. Make sure your ideas are expressed clearly.
8. You should proofread by looking for and correcting grammatical, spelling, and punctuation errors.
9. Students' answers will vary. However, anything the students state that they have learned should have appeared somewhere within their essay.
10. All students, regardless of how well they completed their essays, should be able to find ways to make their writing go more smoothly next time. Students should be able to identify and explain their problem areas in writing.

UNIT NOTE:
Direct the students to use their What Have You Learned answers as a starting point of a discussion within their groups.

UNIT 3 Writing on Your Own

Review It

From the samples that the students have gathered, have each choose one example of each type of writing. Direct students to read each example carefully. Then have them look for common elements found in all three examples. Students may notice that all: explain something or inform about a subject; use facts and examples to support their ideas; have introductions that make the topic and purpose of the essay clear; contain thesis statements in the introductions; develop and support the theses in the body; pull all the main points together in the conclusion.

COOPERATIVE LEARNING STRATEGY:

You can conduct this activity using groups. Provide each group with one sample of each type of expository essay. Have them write a list of common elements of the type they've been assigned. Have the groups share their lists.

Chapter 1
Summarizing a Story
Review It

1. The name of the book is *Roll of Thunder, Hear My Cry.*
2. Important events mentioned in the summary are: Mr. Logan must leave home to work for the railroad; the Logans mortgage their land; a plantation owner gives them trouble; night raids occur; Mrs. Logan loses her job; Mr. Logan breaks his leg; the plantation owner tries to take the farm; the family fights the night raiders; Cassie's uncle brings money to save the farm.
3. The farm is saved.

Lesson 1
Apply It

You may want students to choose from one of the books they have read for class this year or last. Or, you may want to have them choose from a list of books. If the students use books

with which you are familiar, it will be easier to give them guidance and to evaluate their work.

Students should be able to identify clearly the conflict in the book they will be summarizing. They should also be able to fill in at least five events from the story.

Lesson 2
LESSON NOTE: Keep in mind that students have been instructed not to be concerned with grammar and spelling in this lesson. The point is to get their ideas written out.

Apply It

Students' drafting charts should contain the information indicated in the margin on p. 44 of the student book. They should write in full, clear sentences.

Lesson 3
Apply It

Evaluate the students' writing by how well they executed the steps outlined in the revision checklist on p. 35 and p. 46 of the student book. They should also be evaluated against the well-written sample expository essay on p. 21 of the TRM. Finally, evaluate students' essays on their use of grammar, spelling, and punctuation.

Chapter 2
Writing a How-to Explanation
CHAPTER NOTE:
After reading the sample how-to explanation, have students write a list of subjects on which they may want to write their own how-to explanation. Remind them that their essay does not have to be a recipe. Help the students choose a topic which they can explain in three or four paragraphs.

Review It

1. You should shred the cheese or chop it into small pieces.
2. You should spread four tablespoons of sauce on each crust.
3. Sentences that can be underlined are: *People*

can add more seasonings if they like and *Adjust the amount for different numbers of people.*

Lesson 1
Review It
1. He wrote his explanation for friends and younger brothers or sisters.
2. Julio would not have to explain some ingredients that are usually in pizza, how many people the reader will expect to feed, and what pita bread is.
3. Julio would have to explain the other ingredients in the pizza; the cooking tools needed; definitions of certain terms; and how much of each ingredient will be needed.

Apply It
Students should be able to properly identify what each of the two chosen audiences already know and what they will need to be told about the topic. There should be a reasonable explanation of why the audience will want to know certain things.

COOPERATIVE LEARNING STRATEGY:
If students work with partners, have them talk about why one audience may be more appropriate than another (age, interests, etc.). Also have them discuss whether they properly identified the parts of the topic with which their audience will already be familiar and the parts that will need further explanation.

Lesson 2
Review It
It would be difficult to put spices on food already in the broiler. It is easier to do beforehand.

Apply It
Evaluate how well students have identified potential problems with their draft chain and how well they corrected them in the revised chain. Advise students on any missing or confusing steps that they have not corrected before they move on to the next lesson.

Lesson 3
Apply It
To evaluate the students' drafts, note how well they have completed the steps outlined on p. 52 of the student book. Do not evaluate their spelling and grammar at this point.

Lesson 4
Apply It
Evaluate how well the students explain what they set out to. They should also be evaluated against the well-written sample expository essay on p. 21 of the TRM. Students should have included illustrations of steps that would be difficult for their chosen audience to visualize. Note how much of an improvement they have made from their draft essay. Also see that they have responded to the revision checklist on p. 53 of the student book.

Chapter 3
Comparing and Contrasting
Review It
The sentences that should be underlined are: *However, both authors use strange situations and endings that readers do not expect.; Robert Cormier is also an award-winning writer.; Both authors write on subjects that interest teenage readers.; They take their readers into weird situations and make them think about a world without happy endings.*

Apply It
Help students to choose subjects that they can fully compare and contrast in no more than four to five paragraphs.

Lesson 1
Apply It
Students' Venn diagrams should contain information in the individual circles of each subject and within the intersecting section. If not, you may want the students to reconsider the subjects of their essays. There have to be enough similarities and differences between the two subjects for this assignment to be completed properly.

The thesis statements should contain either a comparison or a contrast between the two subjects.

Lesson 2
Apply It
The item-by-item column and the feature-by-feature column should contain the same details. Neither choice of organization is preferable to the other; leave it up to the students. You may want them to write a sentence or two explaining their choices.

Lesson 3
Apply It
Students' essays should reflect the information contained in their Venn diagrams and comparison charts. A well-written draft will have all the elements mentioned in the checklist on p. 58 of the student book. The essays should not switch between a feature-by-feature organization and an item-by-item one.

Lesson 4
Apply It
Evaluate students' essays on how well they have accomplished the tasks listed in the Revision Checklist on p. 59 of the student book. They should also be evaluated against the well-written sample expository essay on p. 21 of the TRM. Essays should show improvement from the original drafts. Note how well students are able to make meaningful comparisons and contrasts. The comparisons and contrasts should not be between trivial or superficial details of the two subjects.

ESL/LEP STRATEGY: To revise their work, pair ESL/LEP students with students fluent in English. The fluent English speakers can help the ESL/LEP students to find wording that makes clear and meaningful comparisons and contrasts. The fluent English speaker will gain a clearer understanding of the revision process by helping another student.

WHAT HAVE YOU LEARNED IN UNIT 3?

1. To introduce a story summary you should name the book and author, state the setting (time and place), and name the major characters.
2. The body of a story summary should include a description of the conflict at the center of the story and an explanation of the most important events in the story.
3. The conclusion of a story summary should include the story's ending, the main idea of the book, or an explanation of what you think the author's message is.
4. The purpose of a how-to explanation is to explain how to do something.
5. You have to know what their background in the subject is, what they already know, and what they need to be told in order to understand your explanation.
6. You should include details that will help your audience successfully complete the project you are explaining, such as what and how much of something they will need and how long they should do something.
7. If steps are out of order or missing, the project cannot be completed correctly or may not work at all.
8. You can make a Venn diagram or comparison chart to see if there are enough similarities and differences between the two subjects to make an interesting and meaningful essay.
9. You should use details that are meaningful, not ones that are trivial or superficial.
10. You can organize the details of your comparison-and-contrast essay feature by feature or item by item.

UNIT NOTE:
You may want to write the tips for the three kinds of writing the students did in this unit on the board or have the students make posters of the tips that can be hung in the classroom for future reference. You can divide the class into three groups and assign one poster to each group.

UNIT 4 Writing on Assignment

Apply It

If students cannot find good examples of expository writing tests, provide them with copies of the well-written sample essay from the Assessment Guide on p. 21 of the TRM.

In looking at how the writers have informed their audiences, students may note that both the research papers and the test essays: grab the reader's attention in the opening sentence; contain a thesis statement in the introductory paragraph; support the thesis in the body of the essay; have a clear purpose; have details arranged in a particular order; pull the main points together, and summarize the main idea or thesis in the conclusion.

Chapter 1
Writing a Test Essay
Review It

1. He tells what a volcano is in the first paragraph.
2. *A volcano forms when rocks melt deep inside the earth.*
3. *A volcano erupts because pressure inside the chamber forces the magma up.*
4. *That upward rush of gas and magma causes the volcanic eruption.*

Lesson 1
Review It

The words and phrases that should be underlined are: *What is; What causes; Why are; answers these questions.*

Lesson 2
Apply It

Students' notes should contain answers to the three questions in the test prompt on p. 64 of the student book. The notes should make some sense when read in the order in which the students have numbered them.

Lesson 3
Apply It

You may want to give students a set time during class to complete their test essays. Call out the time periods noted in Apply It on p. 67 of the student book.

Students should be able to answer test prompt #1 more quickly since they have already planned and organized the information in Lesson 2. To answer test prompt #2, the students will first have to look up the information.

Evaluate students' drafts by how well they followed the steps for drafting as quickly as possible given at the bottom of p. 66 of the student book. However, save your final evaluation using the Assessment Guide until Lesson 4.

Lesson 4
Apply It

Evaluate students on how much they have improved their essay between the draft and final stage. See how well they completed the steps in the revision and proofreading checklists on p. 68 of the student book. To fully evaluate the test essay, use the Assessment Guide from p. 20-24 of the TRM.

The students can compare the approaches they took in answering the essays. Have them discuss any differences to see which approaches worked best. You may ask the students who were less successful in completing the test essay to rewrite their essays using the techniques they learned from the other students.

COOPERATIVE LEARNING STRATEGY:

Have those students who had trouble completing the sample test in the given time write down the problems they ran into. If a number of students became stuck at the same points or with certain aspects of the writing process, have those students work as group with one of the more proficient students on ways to tackle the problem areas of their essays.

Chapter 2
Writing a Research Report
CHAPTER NOTE:

To make this assignment manageable, you may want to assign a few of the classmates' names to each individual or group. Finding the source of each first and last name will require a good deal of research.

Apply It

If students will be working independently, you may not want them to brainstorm ideas with their classmates.

Students' reports can start in numerous manners, such as a quotation by someone famous (or not), an interesting fact, a question, or a statement of the main idea. Encourage students to begin with a sentence that will grab the reader's attention.

Lesson 1
Apply It

Students should feel free to use the sources and questions from Tony's lists on p. 70 of the student book, as well as adding sources and questions of their own.

COOPERATIVE LEARNING STRATEGY:

Have each group share the sources they think of with the other groups. This will give all the groups the opportunity to begin their assignments on an equal footing. It is not necessary for the students to share their lists of questions, since each student or group may be using a different approach.

Lesson 2
Apply It

Remind students to be especially careful about noting the source of each fact, detail, or quotation. Evaluate the students' notes by how well they follow the tips for good note-taking on p. 71 of the student book.

COOPERATIVE LEARNING STRATEGY:

Students within each group should divide the note cards among themselves. Each student can then answer the question or questions assigned to him or her by the group. Another option is for two students to research the same question. One may be able to come up with some information that the other doesn't.

ESL/LEP STRATEGY: This is an excellent opportunity for the students to learn about names and naming traditions in other cultures. You may want to have your ESL students talk to the class about names and naming traditions from their cultures. These students may also be an excellent resource for their group's report.

Lesson 3
Apply It

The thesis statements should clearly explain the main idea and purpose of the essay.

Encourage students to use an organization that is different from the one shown in How to Do It on p. 72 of the student book.

COOPERATIVE LEARNING STRATEGY:

The groups should gather all their notes and decide together on the best outline for the approach of their essay. Students may want to write outlines individually. Then they can take the best elements of the different outlines to use for the group outline.

Lesson 4
Apply It

Students' drafts should incorporate their notes from Lesson 2 and follow the outline they created in Lesson 3. Have students submit both their drafts and final research reports for comparison. There should be a marked improvement between the draft and final version. The final version should show that the students made use of the checklists on p. 73 of the student book. Use the Assessment Guide from p. 20-24 of the TRM to evaluate the final reports.

COOPERATIVE LEARNING STRATEGY:

Each student in a group can be responsible for writing different paragraphs of the report. In that case, students may want to write the paragraphs that correspond to the questions they answered on their note cards.

WHAT HAVE YOU LEARNED IN UNIT 4?

1. A test essay prompt is a question or set of directions.

2. You should look for exactly what the prompt asks or tells you to do.

3. You can quickly organize your thoughts by making an outline of the key steps in answering the prompt and using a cluster diagram of notes on facts and reasons that support your opinion.

4. You should give yourself a few minutes to proofread your essay to make sure no important information is missing and to correct spelling, punctuation, and grammar.

5. You should use your strongest reason first so that if you run out of time, you will have at least presented your best fact, reason, or example to support your thesis.

6. The basic purpose of the research paper is to inform the reader about a subject.

7. Some sources for gathering information are: encyclopedias, books, magazine articles, professional journals, interviews with experts, interviews with others, and computer on-line services.

8. Some tips for good note-taking are: write neatly; use a separate page or card for each note; include every detail possible and don't leave out important facts; keep notes organized and marked in their proper order; write the research question on the top of each page or card; write information in your own words; put direct quotes in quotation marks; record the source of each piece of information.

9. Organizing information in the proper order makes it easier to write your report from your notes without leaving out important information.

10. Revising and proofreading your report gives you the chance to be sure you have completely covered your thesis statement. You are able to make certain you have presented your details clearly and that you have used transitional phrases well. You can be sure that all names and words are spelled correctly and that you have used proper grammar and punctuation.

UNIT NOTE:

You might want to have students compile a list of the areas in which they had the most trouble. Have the students focus on these problems and share their solutions.

For classes that worked as groups, let each group come up with a list of what worked best for them. You might prefer to have the groups that wrote the more informative reports share their lists with the other groups.

UNIT 1 Understanding Description

Apply It

Encourage students to be imaginative when thinking of another place. It needn't be someplace real. Compiling a list of at least five topics will give the student a good variety from which to choose later in the unit.

Chapter 1
Building a Description
Review It

The three parts of a descriptive essay are the introduction, the body, and the conclusion.

Lesson 1
Review It

1. *When was the last time you smiled at someone you passed on the street?*
2. The topic of the description is the Third Avenue Street Fair.
3. *For one day at least, the fair teaches people how to be friendly again.*

Lesson 2
Review It

1. Answers will vary but should focus on a description of a city.
2. Answers will vary but should focus on a description of buildings and perhaps mention the appearance of something odd, if not the gorilla directly.
3. Answers will vary but should focus on a description of the gorilla on the side of the building.
4. The description begins with the scene in the auditorium.
5. Annie zooms in on the governor studying his notes.

Lesson 3
Review It

1. Answers will vary but most students will note that the narrator is reluctant to leave.
2. The writer enjoyed his vacation.
3. Some of the phrases the writer uses to show his feelings are: *hated to leave my winter paradise; one last look at the ocean; the last time I breathed the warm tropical breezes; squawked a sad good-bye.* Details that show his feelings are the way he describes the bay, the rest of his surroundings, and how he tastes the salt water.
4. Students can create a stronger image in a variety of ways, including the addition of details or descriptive language about the setting or by adding words that describe feelings.

Chapter 2
Describing with Style
Apply It

Have students identify the ways in which the descriptions appeal to the audience of each article they collect. Some articles may evoke specific feelings. Some may rely on vivid descriptions of a setting or person. Others may appeal to the reader's senses.

COOPERATIVE LEARNING STRATEGY:

Divide the class into three groups. Assign each group one of the three styles of descriptive writing (sensory details, conveying a mood, and vivid language) discussed in this chapter. Within each group, have the students compare the articles they have collected that use their assigned style. Have them compile a list of common elements found in all the articles. Also have them note if their articles use one of the other styles as well. As you go through each lesson in this chapter, have the group assigned the corresponding topic read their list to the rest of the class.

Lesson 1
Apply It
Students should be able to include at least one detail for each of the five senses. However, encourage students to find at least two details for each.

Lesson 2
Review It
1. The underlined words should be discomfort and annoyance.
2. The underlined words and phrases should include: *same boring scene; just big and loud enough to keep me up; squawk all day long; favorite flying pest; scratching; mosquito bites; peeling sunburn; weeks to wash the sand and salt out.*

Lesson 3
Review It
Students should use very specific words that present a clear, complete, and vivid description of the speakers, cloth, and sounds of the stereo.

Apply It
Note how well the students use vivid language to make their descriptions come to life. Encourage students to use adjectives and adverbs that are specific, evoke feelings, and are complete. See the examples in How to Do It.

ESL/LEP STRATEGY: Before ESL/LEP students write their descriptions, go over the topics they have written in their note books. Help them choose one that will lend itself toward a vivid description. When they have completed their description, have them work with an English-proficient student to help them find the proper words and phrases that will make their descriptions more vivid.

WHAT HAVE YOU LEARNED IN UNIT 1?
1. The goal of descriptive writing is to describe a person, place, or thing in language that brings it to life for the reader.
2. The introduction should get the reader's attention, tell what you are going to describe, and state your impression of your topic.
3. The body should include sensory details that bring your topic to life and that are arranged in a clear order.
4. Your details can be ordered from far to near (general to specific) or from near to far (specific to general).
5. The conclusion should include a restatement of your impression, and end with an image that will stay with your reader.
6. Sensory details help your reader feel or imagine the same things that the character or narrator felt in the place or from the thing being described.
7. Sensory details appeal to the reader's senses.
8. The mood of an essay is how it makes you feel when you read it.
9. Students' answers will vary depending on their chosen subject.
10. To improve your description you should use words that are specific, that appeal to one of the five senses, and that make your description complete by including all the information.

UNIT 2 Writing to Describe

Chapter 1
Planning Your Writing
Apply It

If the students are working individually, have them write down their thoughts as they imagine each step. To help the students focus on the planning stage of writing to describe, ask them to think about such questions as: How would they decide on the topic? Who do they think the intended audience is? Why would they write about such a topic? Where would they gather details they would need to use in their writing? How might they organize their description?

Chapter 1
Planning Your Writing
Apply It

Remind students at the end of each lesson to return to this list.

Lesson 1
Apply It

Students can choose from among the topics they gathered in the Unit 1 opener, or they may want to begin with a new topic. Students may want to make more than one idea branch, then choose among them.

You may want to go over the topics written down by students and guide them in selecting topics with which they can work successfully throughout the rest of the unit. Each student is going to need to write an idea branch about the topic and then narrow its focus, identify the audience for whom he or she will be writing and the goal of the writing, and gather sensory details to expand the description. Students must then be able to organize these details into complete descriptions.

Lesson 2
Apply It

When evaluating the topic webs, be sure that the narrowed topics in the circles are well related to the central idea. Topic webs will vary depending on how narrow or broad the original topic was. However, a well thought out web will contain at least two additional focused topics. Again, you may want to guide each student in the selection of a narrowed topic.

Lesson 3
Apply It

Check that students have identified appropriate audiences for their essays. Also see that they show some knowledge of what the chosen audience can be expected to know before reading the essay. Ask students to explain their final choices of audiences.

COOPERATIVE LEARNING STRATEGY:

If students work with partners, have them discuss why one audience may be more appropriate than another (age, interests, knowledge of the topic, and so on).

Lesson 4
Review It

The underlined details should be: *pleasure; remember; like it much better; years of hard play; satisfying; reminds; reminds me of great moments.*

Apply It

You may want to have students jot down some phrases about their topics with and without describing their feelings. This may help them choose the methods that are best for their topics.

Lesson 5
Apply It

Students should try to think of at least one detail for each sense. However, certain topics may not activate one or more of the senses. For example, many topics may not involve taste.

Lesson 6
Apply It
Students may want to try listing their details using both methods, or using one method in two different ways. They can use trial and error to find out which way works best for their descriptions.

Chapter 2
Developing Your Writing
Apply It
Remind students at the end of each lesson to return to this list.

CHAPTER NOTE:
Keep in mind that in each lesson of this chapter, the students have been told not to be concerned with grammar and spelling. Getting ideas down on paper is their primary goal in this activity. The students are given the opportunity to refine their essays in the following chapter.

Lesson 1
LESSON NOTE:
Encourage students to focus on one detail from their sensory details webs and write a sentence about it. Urge students who have trouble with writing an introduction to move on to Lesson 2. They can start by writing the body of the essay, then return to the introduction. This method may help the students clarify their topics.

Apply It
Students' introductions will vary, but a well-written essay should begin with a sentence that grabs the reader's attention with a question or an interesting detail. The sentence can be followed by a general impression or description of the essay's topic. Students' introductions should reflect the details from their sensory webs from Chapter 1, Lesson 5.

Lesson 2
Apply It
The bodies of the students' essays will vary, but a well-written body will: (1) include details

presented in the order chosen in Chapter 1, Lesson 6; (2) include details that appeal to a reader's senses and bring the topic to life; (3) distinguish what the audience does and does not know about the topic.

Lesson 3
Apply It
The conclusions of the students' essays will vary, but a well-written conclusion should include: (1) a restatement of the overall picture of the topic; (2) perhaps a reference to the writer's feelings; and (3) end with a strong, vivid image or detail.

Chapter 3
Completing Your Writing
Apply It
Remind students at the end of each lesson to return to this list.

Lesson 1
Apply It
Use the checklist provided for the students on p. 34 of the student book and the Assessment Guide on pp. 25-29 of the TRM to evaluate the students' essays.

COOPERATIVE LEARNING STRATEGY:
You may want to assign partners, pairing students of different writing abilities.

ESL/LEP STRATEGY: To revise their work, pair ESL/LEP students with English-proficient students. The proficient English speakers can help the ESL/LEP students to find words that clearly and vividly describe their topics. The English-proficient students will gain a clearer understanding of the revision process by helping other students.

Lesson 2
Apply It
Note how well the students made use of the checklist provided on p. 35 of the student book. You may want to instruct partners to point out the sentences or words that need correction, but

allow the student whose essay is being read to figure out the correct punctuation, grammar, or spelling him- or herself.

ESL/LEP STRATEGY: Have the same pairs of students who worked together in Lesson 1 work together again to proofread their drafts.

Lesson 3
Review It
The strongest and most intriguing of the three titles is *The Ghosts of Opening Day.* This title will best grab the reader's attention.

Apply It
Students' choices of publishing should include a way to reach the audience they chose in Unit 2, Chapter 1, Lesson 3. Encourage students to find and use ways to publish other than those listed. Students may want to write a plan that describes the steps they will follow to have their essays published. Encourage students to follow through with their plans.

WHAT HAVE YOU LEARNED IN UNIT 2?
1. Students' topics should be narrow enough to be covered in an essay of three to five paragraphs in length.
2. A good topic is one that you know well so that you can bring it to life for your readers.
3. In a description, you should use details that appeal to the senses.
4. Introductions should begin with a sentence or question that grabs the reader's interest. The sentence can be followed by a general impression, or description, of the essay's topic.
5. The body of a descriptive essay should include details that appeal to reader's senses and bring the topic to life. These details should be presented in either spatial order or in order of importance.
6. The conclusion of a descriptive essay should include a re-phrasing of the overall picture of the topic and end with a strong, vivid detail. You can also include a statement of your feelings about the topic.
7. When you revise, you make changes to ensure that you have included vivid, clear descriptions. You can add details that produce stronger images. You can improve what you have already written by cutting unnecessary words and clarifying your wording.
8. When you proofread you look for and fix any errors in spelling, grammar, and punctuation.
9. Students' answers will vary depending on their writing experiences in this unit.
10. All students, regardless of how well they completed their essays, should be able to find ways to make their writing go more smoothly next time. Students should be able to identify their problems with writing to describe.

UNIT NOTE:
You may want to write the "Tips for Writing Descriptive Essays" on the chalkboard or have the students make a poster that can be hung in the classroom for future reference.

UNIT 3 Writing on Your Own

Review It

Have each student choose one example of each type of writing from the samples that he or she has gathered. Direct students to read each example carefully. Ask them to look for common elements found in all three examples. Students may notice that all examples use vivid details to describe a given topic.

Then have them look for common elements within each group of examples. They may notice that the event descriptions include a series of actions—people or things in motion. The travel logs include descriptions of places and attempts to familiarize the readers with those locations. The imagery descriptions may all describe things that do not exist or no longer exist.

COOPERATIVE LEARNING STRATEGY:

You can conduct this activity using groups. Provide each group with one sample of each type of expository essay. Have them write a list of common elements of the type they've been assigned. Have the groups share their lists. You can also assign one type of writing to each group and have them find the common elements of that type.

Chapter 1
Describing an Event
Review It

1. The underlined verbs should be: *vibrates; clap; dance; laugh; shout; tap; flutter; drift; sells; fries; serves; is making; is; dips; grills; scoops; displays; eat; talk; laugh; tug; point out; savor; agree; is; is.*
2. Any of the details from the second paragraph in Hank's description appeal to the sense of taste.

Lesson 1
Apply It

Students should be encouraged to think of at least three events for each limb of the idea branch. Guide each student in choosing the event that he or she will use for the rest of this chapter. Ask students to be sure that they have chosen topics they will enjoy writing about and that are meaningful to them. See that the events meet the four criteria listed in What to Do on p. 40 of the student book.

Lesson 2
Apply It

Students should each have at least one answer to each of the questions *who, what, where, when, why,* and *how.* They should also have at least one sensory detail for each of the senses.

Lesson 3
Apply It

Students' planning charts can include some ideas that they cut during this lesson.

The introduction of a well-written plan will: (1) give background information about the event; (2) introduce the topic; (3) include the answers to the *who, what, when, where, why,* and *how* questions; and (4) state the writer's feelings.

The body of the plan will: (1) include details that appeal to the reader's senses; and (2) group details related by sense, subject, or location. At this point, the details do not need to be listed in any particular order.

The conclusion of the plan will: (1) tell the reader the writer's reactions to or feelings about the event; (2) include other sentences that support the writer's reactions or feelings; and (3) perhaps include a re-phrasing of the overall picture of the topic.

Lesson 4
LESSON NOTE:

Before starting their drafts, students may want to review their planning charts to eliminate any information that may detract from the flow of their essays. They may also want to number their groups of details in the order in which they'll be used in the essays.

Apply It

A well-written draft will follow the notes students made in Lesson 2 and Lesson 3. Use the checklists on p. 46 of the student book to evaluate whether students have properly revised and proofread their drafts. Use the Assessment Guide on pp. 25-29 of the TRM to evaluate the final essays.

COOPERATIVE LEARNING STRATEGY:

If students are working with partners, you may want each partner to write a list of the revisions they think the other partner should make. Evaluate how well the student responded to those suggestions and how helpful those suggestions were.

Chapter 2
Writing a Travel Log
Review It

1. The underlined sentence should be: *Oysters may be tasty, but they look gray and slimy.*

2. The underlined sentence should be: *They are puffy and almost round, like doughnuts without holes. They are dusted with powdered sugar and served warm.*

Apply It

Have the students write out their ideas for their trips. They can start with several ideas, then choose the one about which they would most like to write. Some students may choose to write about someplace they've actually been. Some students may want to research places they would like to visit.

Lesson 1
Apply It

Remind students that it's necessary just to get their impressions down on paper. The students' logs should contain notes for at least four or five days of travel. They need not use all of these notes in their essays, though the more information they have to choose from, the more interesting their descriptions will be.

ESL/LEP STRATEGY: This exercise may be diffi-

cult for some students. Some may never have traveled before. Others may have very limited knowledge of the world outside their home-towns. Encourage these students to write about their communities as if they were visiting them for the first time.

This is an excellent opportunity for students from other countries to talk about their homelands. Have them tell the class what a trip to their homeland would be like. Encourage these students to use vivid language, giving them an extra opportunity to practice the tools needed for descriptive writing.

Lesson 2
Apply It

Encourage the students to use a thesaurus. Guide them to notice the subtle differences among words with similar meanings but different connotations. To be sure that students understand the differences, have students mark the words with an *n* for a negative connotation and a *p* for a positive connotation.

ESL/LEP STRATEGY: Pair an ESL/LEP student with an English-proficient student. The English-proficient student can help the ESL/LEP student learn negative and positive connotations.

Lesson 3
Apply It

Check that students have identified appropriate audiences for their essays. See that the audience profiles are complete and well thought out. Note how well students identify what the audience knows, may need to be told, and would be interested in finding out about the students' trips.

Lesson 4
Apply It

The students' drafts of their travel logs can be evaluated according to how well they followed the checklist provided on p. 35 and on p. 51 of the student book and by using the Assessment Guide on pp. 25-29 of the TRM. Also consider the students' use of grammar, punctuation, and spelling in their evaluations.

Chapter 3
Writing an Imaginary Description
Apply It
Remind students not to write about an actual place that they've visited. Encourage students to spend a good amount of time imagining the place and themselves in it. Students should try to use many vivid details in their notes. Have them think about what they would want to tell their friends, classmates, or family about the place that they are imagining.

Lesson 1
Apply It
The student should have several details for all of the senses, even if they are not used in the final essay. The more sensory details the student is able to describe, the more vivid and interesting the essay will be and the more easily the student will be able to describe this imaginary place.

Lesson 2
Review It
The underlined words and phrases should be: *dark waters; observation center; cafeteria; my room; long corridor.*

Apply It
Students may want to organize their notes according to both methods before they decide on which to use. The details they use in either method need not be the same.

Lesson 3
Apply It
Be sure that students have followed the steps in the correct column of the chart on p. 56 of the student book. Note how well the students followed the steps for each part of the essay. Use the checklist on p. 57 of the student book and the Assessment Guide on pp. 25-29 of the TRM to evaluate the drafts and final essays.

COOPERATIVE LEARNING STRATEGY:
Write the students' ideas for titles on the chalkboard as they think of them. Have the class vote on the title of the collection.

After students have read all of the essays written by other students, you may want to have them think of ways to organize the essays into separate chapters of different themes.

WHAT HAVE YOU LEARNED IN UNIT 3?
1. You can ask yourself *who, what , when, where, why*, and *how* questions.
2. You can make a sensory details web.
3. You can group details according to sense, subject, or location.
4. A travel log captures your impressions from a place that you visit.
5. A vivid detail is specific, not general. It appeals to at least one of the five senses. It is complete, with no important piece of information missing.
6. You want to be able to describe a place so that all your readers can understand and experience what you did on your trip.
7. To gather details for an imaginary essay, you can think about yourself in the place, look at pictures or create pictures that suggest the place, play music or other sounds that suggest the place, or pretend that you are there touching, seeing, smelling, tasting things around you. Then make a sensory details web.
8. An imaginary description can be organized as a guided tour (traveling through the place from start to finish), a frozen moment (as if viewing a photograph), or an overall impression (explaining how the place makes you feel).
9. See students' choices of organization in Chapter 2, Lesson 3.
10. Because you are writing about a place no one has been, the audience must rely on you to provide all the information possible so that they can imagine that they are there.

UNIT NOTE:
You may want to write the tips for the three kinds of writing the students did in this unit on the board or have the students make posters of the tips that can be hung in the classroom for future reference. You can divide the class into three groups and assign one poster to each group.

UNIT 4 Writing on Assignment

Apply It

If students cannot find good examples of a descriptive writing test, provide them with copies of the well-written sample essay from the Assessment Guide on p. 26 of the TRM.

Students may notice that most of the test essays begin with a description of what will be expanded in the body, have details grouped by location, subject, or sense in the body, and end with a sentence that sums up what the reader has just read.

Students may also note that, in general, the technical descriptions follow a basic pattern. They all use technical terms, which are defined. They describe the parts of an object and show how each are related to the others. Many of them will be broken up by headings to help the readers find the description of the part about which they'd like to read.

Chapter 1
Writing a Test Essay
Review It

1. Underlined phrases may be: *he has found paradise; he would like to live there; an escape from hectic modern life; peaceful and calm; "summer evenings were twice as long"; life was much more relaxed.*
2. The underlined phrase should be *For Charley.*
3. The underlined phrase should be *as people do now.*
4. Details that appeal to the sense of hearing are: *Evenings are quiet; no noisy cars or roaring planes; no humming air conditioners; People talk quietly.*
5. A detail that appeals to the sense of sight is *fireflies flicker.*
6. Charley's overall reaction to Galesburg is that he would rather live there than in the present.

Lesson 1
Apply It

The underlined phrases should be: *Describe the house; describe the neighborhood around it; Include details; show how the family pretends to feel.*

Lesson 2
Apply It

Students' notes on either test prompt should include brief jotted notes or an outline, with related details grouped together. They should also include a sensory details web. Those who use the second prompt may be able to include more details since they will be describing a place that they know well.

Lesson 3
Apply It

You may want to give students a set time during class to complete their test essays. Have them read the tips in How to Do It beforehand. Call out the time periods noted in Apply It on p. 65 of the student book. Have students submit both their notes from Lesson 2 and the drafts of the test essays. Evaluate their work based on how well they followed the steps outlined on p. 65 of the student book.

Lesson 4
Apply It

Evaluate students' essays using the Assessment Guide on pp. 25-29 of the TRM and on: (1) how well the students answered the prompt; (2) the completeness and clarity of their descriptions; (3) their use of sensory details; (4) the use of introductory words to clarify their answers to the prompt; and (5) their use of correct grammar, punctuation, and spelling.

COOPERATIVE LEARNING STRATEGY:

Some students may have trouble completing the sample test in the time given. Have those students write down the problems they ran into as they tried to complete their essays. Were there a number of students who had trouble at the same points or with certain aspects of the writing process? Have those students work as a group with one or more proficient students on ways to tackle the problem areas of their essays.

Chapter 2
Writing a Technical Description
Review It

1. A CD player is described.

2. The three main parts are the disc tray, the disc selector, and the playback.

3. Technical terms (terms which are defined) include disc tray, open/close button, and disc selector buttons.

4. The disc tray holds the compact discs to be played. The open/close button opens and closes the tray. The disc selector button allows you to choose the disc to be played.

5. The underlined words and phrases should be: *on the far right; to the left of the play button; below the play and stop buttons; on the right; on the left; on the front of the player.*

Apply It

Students should collect at least four technical descriptions to give them a clear idea of how they are written. Below each description in their notebooks, have the students jot some notes about what each description explains. Guide students in their choices of topics so that they choose one that they can cover successfully in three to five paragraphs.

COOPERATIVE LEARNING STRATEGY:

Divide the class into small groups of no more than four students. Assign each student one of the roles listed below. Then have the group brainstorm a list of ideas from which they will select their topic. Monitor the groups to ensure that all students contribute ideas.

ORGANIZER: Will lead the discussions in each lesson.

DESIGNER: Makes the technical drawing of the subject of the description.

TECHNICAL WRITER: Writes the final result of the discussions and collaborative efforts of the group.

RECORDER: Records and organizes information presented during the discussions.

All members of the group should participate in the discussions. Cooperation among group members is essential for the success of the assignment. The goals will be the same as those of an individual student completing this project.

Though tasks have been assigned to specific team members, all members should feel free to contribute ideas and offer suggestions for improvement for all phases of this project. Each member of the group should pre-read the lesson and come prepared with any ideas or necessary notes.

Lesson 1
Apply It

Students can use the Audience Profile Chart on p. 102 of the TRM.

Students' audience profile charts should show that they've thought about and answered the questions in What to Do on p. 69 of the student book. The charts should also reflect that an effort has been made to match what the audience needs and wants to know and the details the students will describe.

COOPERATIVE LEARNING STRATEGY:

The entire group should be responsible for deciding who the target audience is, what the audience needs to know, and which features will be described.

Lesson 2
Apply It

Students' planning charts will vary depending on their topic. However, they should follow the general organization described in What to Do and shown in the sample chart in How to Do It on p. 70 of the student book. See that students' plans contain enough details in the body to produce a useful technical description in Lessons 4 and 5.

COOPERATIVE LEARNING STRATEGY:

The recorder writes the group's ideas for each part of the essay on separate sheets of paper. The writer can coordinate the assembled notes into the final planning chart.

Lesson 3
Apply It
Students may want to make word webs for each detail to be described.

COOPERATIVE LEARNING STRATEGY:
The entire team should brainstorm the features and descriptions to be used. The recorder can make word webs as the group comes up with descriptions for each of the details of their product. The writer will be responsible for writing the final chart for the technical terms. The designer may want to make some quick sketches of the details that will be described.

ESL/LEP STRATEGY: ESL/LEP students may be unfamiliar with many more of the terms to be used than would their intended audience. Have the ESL/LEP student keep a list of unfamiliar words and phrases. Then pair the ESL/LEP student with an English-proficient student. The English-proficient student can explain which words would be commonly understood by the audience and can help the ESL/LEP student learn the meanings of unfamiliar words and phrases.

Lesson 4
Apply It
Students' drafts should incorporate their notes from their audience profile charts in Lesson 1, their planning charts in Lesson 2, and use the technical terms and descriptions from Lesson 3. Use the checklist on p. 72 of the student book to evaluate the quality of the students' drafts. Students may want to make a number of sketches from which they can choose to make a final drawing in the next lesson.

COOPERATIVE LEARNING STRATEGY:
The designer should draw sketches from two or three angles to see which works best for displaying the features described. The group should choose the final design. The writer should use the recorder's notes, the audience profile chart in Lesson 1, the planning chart from Lesson 2, and the technical term chart from Lesson 3 to draft the technical description.

Another approach you may want to use is to have each student in a group be responsible for writing different paragraphs of the description.

Lesson 5
Apply It
Have students submit both their drafts and final technical descriptions for comparison. There should be a marked improvement between the drafts and final versions. The final versions should show that the students made use of the checklists on p. 73 of the student book. Use the Assessment Guide from p. 25-29 of the TRM to evaluate the final descriptions.

Be generous in viewing the art. Not all students have talent in that area. However, the drawings should include and clearly show all features described in the descriptions.

COOPERATIVE LEARNING STRATEGY:
Have one group act as a sample audience for another. The recorder should write down the ideas and suggestions from the sample audience.

Afterward, the writer should revise and proofread. The rest of the group can give proofreading and revision suggestions for the final description. The designer should submit the final art and layout to the group.

The designer should incorporate any suggested changes to the sketches before making the final drawing.

WHAT HAVE YOU LEARNED IN UNIT 4?

1. A test essay prompt is a question or set of directions.

2. You should look for exactly what the prompt asks or tells you to do.

3. You can quickly organize your thoughts by making an outline of the key steps in answering the prompt and using a cluster diagram of notes on facts and reasons that support your opinion.

4. You should give yourself a few minutes to revise your essay to make sure no important information is missing and to correct spelling, punctuation, and grammar.

5. Skipping lines in your draft gives you space to make changes in the revision stage of the writing process.

6. A technical description shows a reader the parts of an object, describes those parts, and shows how they are related.

7. The key elements of a technical description are: visual aids that increase the audience's understanding; headings that break the information into small parts; descriptive details about the object; details that increase the audience's understanding; technical terms; and explanations of terms that the audience might not know.

8. You want to help the audience understand what you describe, so you must understand what they will want and need to know.

9. The chart showing the audience's needs helps you identify what the audience needs to know and match it with the details you will need to include.

10. Most people are not familiar with the specific meanings of the technical terms. You always want to keep your audience in mind.

UNIT NOTE:

You might want to have students compile a list of the areas in which they had most trouble. Have the students focus on these problems and share their solutions. Also encourage students to discuss the parts of writing they enjoyed most.

For classes that worked as groups, let each group come up with a list of what worked best in their group. Then you can compile a class tips list from these. You might prefer to have the groups that wrote the more successful descriptions share their lists with the other groups.

UNIT 1 Understanding Sentences

Unit Opener
1. Students should note that each sentence expresses a complete thought and can stand alone.
2. Students should note that some sentences should have different punctuation while others should have information added.
3. Answers will vary.

ESL/LEP STRATEGY: Every language contains units of thought, although they may look quite different from English sentences. Ask ESL students to talk about how units of thought look or act in their native language. They might wish to talk about punctuation, word order, or other language elements.

UNIT NOTE: Tell students that they should fill out the first two columns of the chart with what they already know and what they want to learn about sentences. At the end of the unit, ask students to return to this chart and fill out the third column with what they learned in the unit. You might consider using this chart in individual conferences with students. If students have not learned all of the information they wanted to learn, suggest that they consult the Table of Contents on pages iii–iv or A Guide to Writers: Terms to Know on pages 122–124 for related topics.

Keep in mind that the activities on this page are intended to establish prior knowledge, not to act as a test of information learned. You might consider asking students to return to this page at the end of the unit and to discuss the answers to questions 1 and 2 again, in light of what they learned in their work in the unit. The answers they give before and after completing the unit can serve as an assessment of their learning.

Chapter 1
Identifying the Purposes of Sentences
Answers will vary. Examples:
1. Declarative: *We are going to the store.*
2. Interrogative: *Are you going to the store?*
3. Imperative: *Go to the store.*
4. Exclamatory: *Go to the store now!*
5. Discussions should identify the different purposes of the sentences and when each should be used.

Lesson 1
Declarative Sentences
1. Chickens are soaring through the air. The roofs of houses are flying down the streets. Now the announcer is talking. That's right.
2. The declarative sentences simply make a statement.
3. Descriptions should include only declarative sentences.

Lesson 2
Interrogative Sentences
Answers will vary, but should be interrogative sentences. Examples:
1. Did Leann put her diamond necklace on the dresser?
2. When is the first day of spring?
3. Does that book have a surprise ending?
4. Students should name a well-known person.
5. Questions may include: Where were you born? What is your most important accomplishment? When did you decide on a career?

Lesson 3
Imperative Sentences
1. Please stop making that noise.
2. Tanisha, stop watching so much TV.
3. Win the tournament.
4. Directions should contain imperative sentences.

Lesson 4
Exclamatory Sentences
Answers will vary.
1. You're swerving into his lane! (sense of urgency)
2. The concert's sold out. (no urgency)
3. You make me furious! (sense of urgency)
4. Some sentences in students' stories should be exclamatory.

Chapter 1
Wrap-Up

1. Paragraph 1: D, In, D, D, Ex
paragraph 2: D, D, In
paragraph 3: D, Im, D, D
2. Students should include correct end punctuation and label each sentence with the correct purpose.

COOPERATIVE LEARNING STRATEGY: Have small groups of students take turns reading different types of sentences aloud while other group members try to identify whether each sentence is declarative, interrogative, imperative, or exclamatory.

CHAPTER NOTE: Students have been asked in the Apply It sections of this chapter to write in three of the four modes of writing: narration, exposition, and description. They will be asked to write persuasively in future lessons in this book. To help students clarify the requirements of each mode, direct them to The Modes of Writing on page 119 of their book.

Chapter 2
Recognizing Sentence Structure

1. Answers will vary. Example: She tossed the anchor overboard as we finally reached the island. We sang, we danced, and we celebrated. The captain and the first mate both gave speeches. It was only when we stopped celebrating that we noticed that the boat had drifted away from the island.
2. Students should note how the changes they made helped make the paragraph smoother and easier to follow.

Lesson 5
Subjects and Predicates

1. <u>Edward</u> looked into the black cave gloomily.
2. <u>No one</u> saw the thief escape.
3. Dive off the high diving board into the pool.
4. Students should underline complete subjects once and complete predicates twice in their own writing.

LESSON NOTE: Reinforce the identification of subjects and predicates by asking several students to write a sentence from their own writing on the board. Ask other students to then underline the subjects and predicates.

Lesson 6
Simple Sentences

Answers will vary. Examples:
1. The cat ate his dinner.
2. The cat ate his dinner and played with a string.
3. The cat and the dog ate their dinners and slept peacefully.

Lesson 7
Compound Sentences

Possible answers:
1. The calf whimpered, and the wolves drew closer.
2. The game was close; however, we finally won.
3. Answers will vary. Example: In 1954, a businessman visited a restaurant and liked what he saw. He bought that restaurant and tried something different. He set up a new system so that his workers could make hamburgers, milkshakes, and French fries very quickly. The idea caught on so well that when he died in 1984, there were more than 750,000 restaurants in his chain.

Lesson 8
Complex Sentences

1. S, CX, CD, CX, CX
2. Students should correctly label the types of sentences they use.

ESL/LEP STRATEGY: Pair ESL/LEP students with an English-proficient peer to work on the concepts of dependent and independent clauses. Have the students take turns reading aloud the examples in Lessons 7–8. Ask them to explain which kind of clause each one is and how they made their choice. Then ask ESL/LEP students to construct two examples of each type of clause.

COOPERATIVE LEARNING STRATEGY: Have small groups of students write a round-robin story. Before they begin, have students write the words *simple, compound,* and *complex* on 10 or more strips of paper. Then have students draw strips and add that type of sentence to the story.

Chapter 2
Wrap-Up

1. Answers will vary. Example: You've used paper cups; you've probably used them a thousand times. A man named Hugh Moore, who invented the paper cup, didn't care about the cup, though. He had a different idea. He wanted to sell drinks of water. In 1908, Hugh Moore built a vending machine made of porcelain. Although he designed a paper cup to hold the water, nobody bought the water. Later, Moore realized that he could sell just the cups. That was a smashing success, and today, paper cups are a huge business.
2. Students should correctly label the kinds of sentences they use.

Chapter 3
Constructing Sentences

Answers will vary. Examples:
1. They went with us because they were our friends.
2. When we did our jobs, they helped us.
3. They left the dog there because they forgot about it.
4. After the rider looked down the street, the bicycle zoomed away.
5. His friend, who was wearing a toolbelt, borrowed a hammer.
6. Students should discuss why they made revisions and how their revisions changed the meanings of the sentences.

Lesson 9
Phrases

1. <u>With all our packing done,</u> we left <u>for the airport.</u>
2. We hoped <u>to explore space.</u>
3. <u>Finding no chocolate,</u> we ate licorice.
4. <u>To be honest,</u> we are leaving.
5. Student writing should include a variety of phrases.

Lesson 10
Misplaced Modifiers

1. With a growl, the lion jumped on the man.
2. With a smile, the state trooper said he had a few problems.

3. The theater, built 100 years ago, creates a good impression on visitors.
4. Carlo, who is Anna's brother, called for directions.
5. Answers will vary. Example:
   With a grin, Alby stared at him in disbelief. "You can't mean she just let the ducks go?"
   "Why, yes," Barney, who was watching the ducks, said. "She simply opened the cage and out they went, quacking loudly."
   "I wanted to take pictures of them from the north end of their pen," Alby said. "Oh, well. They'll be famous anyway. Newspapers all over the country will carry the story of the escaping ducks."

ESL/LEP STRATEGY: The placement of modifiers and the words to which they refer differs from language to language. Pair ESL/LEP students with an English-proficient peer to review the rules for the placement of modifiers in English. Then have them complete exercises 1–4 together.

Lesson 11
Dangling Modifiers

Answers will vary. Examples:
1. After we read books all afternoon, the light finally dimmed.
2. The boy picked up the apple that was rolling on the ground.
3. Because I was not able to run a computer, a hacker walked over and helped me.
4. Answers will vary. Example: After we waited for hours, the snow began. The snow was soft and fluffy, and the children flung it into the air, squealing with happiness. Although I was only a small boy, my father expected me to stop playing and to shovel.

Lesson 12
Sentence Fragments

Answers will vary. Examples:
1. I did it because you told me to.
2. I love my old house on the street with the cherry trees.
3. Whenever I think about my first dance, I laugh.
4. We got angry thinking about the waste of time.
5. Clothing descriptions should contain no sentence fragments.

Lesson 13
Run-on Sentences

1. Answers will vary. Example: Rob Roy was the Scottish Robin Hood. He lived from 1671 to 1734. He was called Rob because it is the Scottish word for "red" and he had red hair. When he was 22, Roy became head of the MacGregor clan and inherited huge estates. When they were taken from him, he became an outlaw, stealing cattle. Roy was arrested and imprisoned in London. The famous book Rob Roy, by Sir Walter Scott, was based on his life. Rob Roy's life was also the basis for a movie.
2. Movie reviews should not contain run-on sentences.

Lesson 14
Comma Faults
Answers will vary. Examples:
1. He played baseball, and he played basketball.
2. One way is easy; the other way is hard.
3. She ran; there was no other way to escape.
4. Student writing should contain comma faults that are then corrected.

Lesson 15
Wordiness and Rambling
Answers will vary. Examples:
1. The red car is in the lot behind the house.
2. He did not offer much guidance.
3. He said it, and then he said it again.
4. We will go as soon as he is ready.
5. While we were in the sailboat, we began to realize we needed to cooperate to survive. The water was rising higher in the boat every minute. We also knew that although a boat had come by last night at 7:30, we might not see another boat for hours.

COOPERATIVE LEARNING STRATEGY: Divide the class into small groups. Give each group a 15-minute limit to write as many examples of wordiness and redundancy as they can. Compare lists at the end of this time and compile a class list of wordy expressions and their concise counterparts to post in the classroom. Encourage students to review the list periodically and eliminate these expressions when they revise their work.

Lesson 16
Parallelism
Answers will vary. Examples:
1. Marge squirmed, lied, and tried to pretend it never happened.
2. Our tasks are to watch, to listen, and to learn what we can.
3. First Matt went to the dentist, then he went to the bakery, and then he went to school.
4. The software doesn't work, and it is disappointing everyone.
5. Students should use parallelism correctly in at least three sentences.

Chapter 3
Wrap-Up
Answers will vary. Example:
1. The right bike can cost at least $200. Often, shopping makes it easier to choose the best bike for the money. If you spend that $200, for example, you can expect to buy a sturdy frame, a wide seat, multiple gears, and a shock-absorbing suspension. All of those features can help you get a bike that is comfortable, rides well, and serves you for many years. A bike is a big purchase, so you should shop wisely.

   These hints make it clear why it is good to buy a bike from a buying guide. According to the buying guide, you should know the kind of bike you want, decide on the key features important to you, and keep your price range in mind.
2. Students should correct their errors in the topics discussed in this chapter.

Unit 1
What Have You Learned?
1. F
2. F
3. T
4. T
5. T
6. C
7. D
8. E
9. A
10. B

11. F

Answers will vary. Example:

12. Talk to me before we go.

13. When we went, we had nothing.

14. They left early, ate little, and drank nothing.

15. The chess player scowled while his opponent grinned.

16. Conditions were dangerous; he could not leave.

17. A friendly nod from his friend pleased the man.

UNIT NOTE: The problems addressed in this unit are some of the more common errors students make when constructing sentences. Ask students to review writing they have done—either with or without your comments—and identify the areas in which they consistently make the errors referred to in this unit. Then have students construct their own "editor's checklist" by listing their most common errors and posting that list inside their assignment notebook. They should consult this list every time they revise their work and add to it as needed.

Many of your students may be familiar with the steps of the writing process. To review these steps with the class or to clarify the process, direct students to "The Writing Process," on page 120 of their book.

UNIT 2 Building Sentences

Unit Opener

1. Students should note that each sentence expresses a complete thought and can stand alone.
2. Students should note the errors in grammar, mechanics, and usage.
3. Answers will vary.

UNIT NOTE: Tell students that they should fill out the first two columns of the chart with what they already know and what they want to learn about sentences. At the end of the unit, ask students to return to this chart and fill out the third column with what they learned in the unit. You might consider using this chart in individual conferences with students. If students have not learned all of the

information they wanted to learn, suggest that they consult the Table of Contents on pages iii–iv or A Guide to Writers: Terms to Know on pages 122–124 for related topics.

Keep in mind that the activities on this page are intended to establish prior knowledge, not to act as a test of information learned. You might consider asking students to return to this page at the end of the unit and to discuss the answers to questions 1 and 2 again, in light of what they learned in their work in the unit. The answers they give before and after completing the unit can serve as an assessment of their learning.

Chapter 4
Understanding Grammar

1. *Show* refers to a television program.
2. *Show* means to exhibit or display something.
3. *Show* refers to musical theater.

ESL/LEP STRATEGY: Understanding how words can take on different functions in a sentence is sometimes difficult for ESL/LEP speakers. Have these students work with proficient English speakers to create a list of other words that function as different parts of speech in different circumstances.

Crossword puzzles often use clues that do not specify a part of speech. Thus, the clue "bear" might refer to an animal (noun) or to an act of endurance (verb). Students might use these puzzles, which are available in many newspapers and magazines, to reinforce this idea.

Lesson 17
Nouns

1. half-light (CM), Lolly (P), sign (C), "Danger!" (C), half-brother (CM), Jim (P), edge (C), Black Gulch (P, CM), Lolly (P), tree (C), seconds (C), Jim (P), hands (C), help (C)
2. Students should underline the nouns in their writing.

Lesson 18
Verbs

1. braced, heard, was, could catch, was, was passing, looked, crossed, threw
2. Students should underline the verbs they have used and should use verbs that show action.

Lesson 19
Pronouns

1. he, his, him, they
2. Mim wanted <u>her</u> speech to be perfect, so <u>she</u> practiced and practiced <u>it</u>. Finally, when Mim stood up before the club, <u>she</u> smiled. Mim knew <u>she</u> was about to give the best speech of <u>her</u> life.

Lesson 20
Adjectives

1. sweet/smell; South American/meadow; yellow/sundews; deadly/trap; gluey/nectar; poisonous/substance; sundew/plants; beautiful and deadly/plants; many/kinds
2. Students should use adjectives that clearly describe what they see outside.

Lesson 21
Adverbs

1. (The adverbs are underlined.)
<u>Slowly</u>/advanced; moved/<u>carefully</u>; hooted/<u>noisily</u>; <u>Somehow</u>/seemed; <u>deathly</u>/afraid; <u>Everywhere</u>/went; <u>always</u>/followed; <u>really</u>/getting
2. Answers will vary. Example:
   <u>Just ahead</u>, Sarah saw the finish line <u>clearly</u>. It <u>really</u> hurt to breathe, but she told herself that <u>somehow</u> she could keep going. This race was <u>very</u> important. If she came in first, her school would <u>easily</u> win the championship. <u>Unfortunately</u>, if she did not, she would be <u>largely</u> responsible for the defeat.
   <u>Unhappily</u>, out of the corner of her eye, Sarah saw someone behind her. It was <u>almost certainly</u> Bethany, the girl from East High. Bethany ran <u>very quickly</u>. Sarah heard the footfalls. She began to run just as <u>quickly</u>. Every step hurt <u>terribly</u>, but Sarah kept going. <u>Somehow</u>, she would win.
3. Students should underline the adverbs they use and be prepared to discuss how using adverbs changed the story.

ESL/LEP STRATEGY: Reinforce for ESL/LEP speakers that one way to identify many adverbs is through their -*ly* ending. Ask ESL/LEP students to make a list of adverbs that end in -*ly* and use them

in sentences. Stress that these adverbs often follow the verbs they modify.

Lesson 22
Prepositions

1. <u>In the morning</u>, when Thom opened his eyes, he realized <u>with a start</u> that he was late <u>for his job</u>. He raced <u>down the stairs</u>, grabbed his coat, and sped <u>out the door</u>. <u>With luck</u>, he could stay <u>during the evening</u> and finish his work.
2. Students should underline the prepositions they find in the chosen paragraph.

Lesson 23
Conjunctions

1. and, but
2. and
3. Because
4. or
5. but, because
6. Because
7. When
8. and
9. and
10. because
11. Answers will vary. Example:
    In the 1800s, people became interested in ancient temples and pyramids. Some traveled to Egypt and tried to bring treasures back. Some of the visitors were archaeologists, but others were bounty hunters. They wanted the treasures and mummies to sell.
    Today, archaeologists find few treasures because most have been found and some have been stolen. Many of the ancient temples remain, however, and they still amaze visitors.
12. Students should underline the conjunctions they use.

Lesson 24
Interjections

Answers may vary. Possible answers:
1. Wow!
2. Great!
3. What?
4. Stop,

5. Oh, no!

6. Answers will vary. Interjections should be used correctly in student writing.

Chapter 4
Wrap-Up

1. Answers will vary. Example:

"Hey! Either I'm crazy, or that's a bear by those dumpsters," Esther said. "Wow!" Slowly the bear came closer to where the two girls stood, telling themselves it might go away.

"It's coming closer, but I know we're in no danger," Esther told her friend Sue. Esther knew the bear was as scared of them as they were of it. But still, it was scary.

They waited while the bear walked by them. Esther held her breath. "It's gone. Are you all right?" she said to her friend. "That was a close one."

2. Student writing should correctly identify all eight parts of speech.

COOPERATIVE LEARNING STRATEGY: Divide the class into an even number of small groups. Have the groups create fill-in-the-blank stories that call for different parts of speech. The groups should label each blank with the required part of speech. Then have groups exchange stories and fill in the blanks. Ask the groups to read their finished stories aloud to the class.

Chapter 5
Using the Parts of Speech

1. That was the <u>worst</u> movie I've ever seen.

2. We <u>went</u> to the movies last Thursday.

3. <u>He</u> and <u>I</u> bought popcorn without butter.

4. We got the <u>best</u> seats in the theater—front row!

5. Do you think <u>we</u> could go again next week?

6. Students should show an understanding of the errors in the sentences.

Lesson 25
Basic Verb Tenses

1. <u>will walk</u>; future

2. <u>decided</u>; past

3. <u>is</u>; present

4. <u>does</u>; present

5. Students should revise their sentences so that they use the three basic tenses.

Lesson 26
Regular Verbs

1. visited

2. will apply

3. have interviewed

4. is calling

5. decide

6. Students should use each verb tense at least once and label the tenses correctly.

Lesson 27
Irregular Verbs

1. sang

2. gone

3. took, or takes; saw, or sees

4. knew; saw

5. When he <u>saw</u> that opera star, he <u>knew</u> she was something special. She <u>wore</u> a beautiful white gown and <u>stood</u> up there like a queen. Then she <u>began</u> to sing. She <u>sang</u> like an angel. Later, when we had <u>gone</u> from the theater, I <u>saw</u> her leave. She <u>blew</u> me a kiss.

LESSON NOTE: Reinforce to students that they know many irregular verbs simply by speaking the language. Also mention that irregular verbs are often sticking points even for proficient speakers. (Examples: *brang, throwed*.) Caution students to double-check a verb in a dictionary if they aren't sure of how to form its tenses. You might also ask students to make a class list of additional irregular verbs to complement the list in this lesson. Post this list where students can easily consult it.

Lesson 28
Verb Tense Consistency

Answers will vary. Examples:

1. told or tells; did or does

2. heated or heats; put or will put

3. fried; walked

4. sang; watched

5. I took a tour of a newspaper office last month. While I was there, I <u>saw</u> reporters bustling about, working on a story about a beached whale. They talked fast and <u>walked</u> faster. Photographers <u>were</u> rushing about, too, showing me lots of great pictures. I got wrapped up in the excitement, and for a while, I really <u>wanted</u> to be a newspaper reporter myself.

ESL/LEP STRATEGY: Tell ESL/LEP students to check their use of tenses by verbalizing *when* the action that they are writing about happened or will happen. Identifying when an action happened can help students assign the correct tense.

Lesson 29
Direct and Indirect Objects
1. Someday we will cruise <u>the Indian Ocean</u>.
2. Before you rig <u>the sails</u>, please give <u>Barney</u> <u>the end of the rope</u>.
3. He wrote <u>Seven Years Before the Mast</u>.
4. She sailed <u>that boat</u> and never gave <u>anyone</u> <u>trouble</u>.
5. Should I lend <u>them</u> <u>my new boat</u>?
6. Jackson tried to show <u>the crew</u> <u>the ropes</u>, but they ignored <u>him</u>.
7. We called <u>the sailor</u> Mr. Danger after he told <u>us</u> the <u>story</u>. He said it was a calm <u>night</u> at sea when suddenly an angry shark began hitting <u>the boat</u> again and again. Before long, panicked sailors threw <u>themselves</u> <u>into</u> <u>lifeboats</u>. That, of course, only made <u>things</u> worse.
8. Student writing should correctly use and identify indirect and direct objects.

Lesson 30
Subject and Object Pronouns
1. we
2. He and I
3. her and me
4. Jim and I
5. her
6. you and me
7. Let Gene and me tell you and her about poodles. First, when he and <u>I</u> went to Europe last year, <u>he</u> and I found out that poodles first came from Germany. Did you know that? Also, a poodle breeder told <u>him</u> and <u>me</u> that

there are three kinds of poodles: toy, miniature, and standard.

LESSON NOTE: To grasp this lesson, students need a clear understanding of the difference between subjects and objects. You might review with them the examples printed on torn paper in this lesson. Have them identify each subject and object pronoun and give reasons for their choices. Then have them construct their own sentences using the pronouns in the chart as a guide.

Lesson 31
Adjectives and Adverbs that Compare
1. nicest
2. better
3. Students should use the three comparative forms of adverbs and adjectives correctly.

LESSON NOTE: Adjectives and adverbs of two or more syllables may take the words *more* and *most* in comparisons; they may also add the suffixes *-er* or *-est*. Tell students that if they are unsure, the best course is to try both methods to see which sounds better, or to check a dictionary.

Lesson 32
Subject-Verb Agreement
1. chef and owner; are planning
2. Fred; fries
3. Some; are planning
4. Ms. Polumbo and I; decorate
5. workers; forget
6. class; cooks
7. told; get; knew; go; said; looked; said
   Students should use correct subject-verb agreement in their story ending.

Lesson 33
Pronoun Agreement
1. her
2. them
3. his or her
4. him or her
5. he; her
6. Answers will vary. Example:
   The class had planned <u>its</u> trip for months. Now everyone was so excited that <u>no one</u> could calm down. Some people got out <u>their</u> maps. A few people did a last minute check of their tickets.

Francie and Tim sat by <u>themselves</u> and looked at the pictures of Brazil. Both were thinking that they were lucky to be going on such a trip.

<u>It</u> was a good group, and <u>it</u> had worked hard, Francie thought. The members of the class were on their way.

Lesson 34
Clear Pronoun Reference
Answers may vary. Examples:
1. The astronomer wrote to the student before the astronomer became famous.
2. We trust the star chart and the telescope, but the star chart sometimes lets us down.
3. If Jan and Sally are late, the reason will be that Sally had to watch the comet.
4. Answers may vary. Examples:

   Comets were omens of doom in ancient times; they even appeared in ancient <u>people's</u> tapestries. Two of the best known comets are Halley's and Hale-Bopp. <u>They</u> are a dramatic sight—there the <u>comets</u> are, sparkling in the sky. It is thrilling to see <u>them</u>.

Chapter 5
Wrap-Up
1. Answers will vary. Example:

   Jake and I set off for our jungle adventure with our guide. We think he is the best guide we have ever used. The scariest thing in the entire trip happened right away. Jake and I saw the largest snake we had ever seen gliding toward us. It moved really slowly, and then it flicked its tongue.

   "Quick! Move!" our guide told us, and Jake and I did. Another second and there would have been nothing we could have done. That snake would have been on top of Jake and me.

   After that, though, the trip went smoothly. We saw colorful birds, the most beautiful birds we had ever seen. Jake and I will remember that trip for the rest of our lives.
2. Students should correctly use the parts of speech.

CHAPTER NOTE: This chapter contains some of the trickiest issues in the English language.

To give students extra practice with these issues, divide the class into groups and have each group compile a chapter test. Have groups trade tests and complete them to discover what aspects of this chapter they still have trouble with. Then assign groups to construct a lesson about the issue and to present their lesson to the class.

Chapter 6
Understanding Mechanics
1. I liked the first book with Nancy Drew as the detective, which was called *The Secret of the Old Clock.*
2. Tim's mom only likes to read biographies.
3. Everyone who is a good reader knows where the library is.
4. Sharma should read that book about wild animals.
5. Students should have reasons for the changes they made in the sentences.

ESL/LEP STRATEGY: Mechanics vary from language to language. In Spanish, for example, interrogative sentences begin and end with a question mark; in German, nouns are capitalized; and because Japanese does not use an alphabet, its mechanical issues are completely different from those of English. You might wish to pair an ESL/LEP student with a proficient English speaker for this entire chapter, so that the ESL/LEP student may have extra practice on these issues.

Mechanics also vary within a language. These variations can be seen in comparing different style sheets. For example, some style sheets capitalize all words in titles and some write out only numbers under ten. This book was written with *The Chicago Manual of Style.* If your school has a style sheet, you might wish to compare its treatment of the issues in this chapter with this book's treatment of them. You might then adjust your lessons accordingly.

Lesson 35
Capitalization
1. If; South Dakota; let
2. Yesterday; Maura; I; eastern
3. The; We
4. The; Grand Canyon; Japanese
5. The; Gobi Desert

6. Travelers; Southwest; Santa Fe; New Mexico
7. Although; North Star; north
8. My; Mr. Gerson; you
9. Students should use capitalization appropriately.

Lesson 36
Periods
1. Yesterday, Dr. D.L. Grane, an M.D. from St. Paul, left the United States. When U.S. government officials heard about this, they went to his P.O. box. In it was a letter postmarked NY and addressed to his partner, Dr. M. Berger.
2. Students should use periods correctly.

Lesson 37
Question Marks and Exclamation Points
Answers may vary. Example:
1. Oh, no! Look at this! Bucky, did you do this? I know that expression. Bucky, you are a bad dog. Come here this instant! I know you must have been hungry, but that's no reason to get into the garbage. It's a mess! What were you thinking? Don't cower in the corner like that. Don't you know the trouble you've caused me? The whole team is coming over here for a party in ten minutes. That's right, ten minutes! I wish you were a person. Then I would make you clean all this up.
2. Students should show an understanding of the correct use of question marks and exclamation points.

Lesson 38
Commas
1. We have oranges, trail mix, and sandwiches in our backpacks.
2. On top of this mountain and the other one, there is a lodge.
3. Before I head down, let me put on my goggles.
4. The instructor and his student skied down the bumpy slope.
5. During World War II, a group of men who became known as the 10th Mountain division trained in the Colorado mountains. According to the history books, they learned to ski, shoot, and survive outdoors in freezing weather.

Later, they were pioneers in the ski industry and helped to make the sport popular.

Lesson 39
Semicolons
1. He made pasta, which was delicious; salad, which tasted like weeds; and dessert, which was a blueberry pie.
2. We came to dinner late; no one noticed.
3. Forget the wilted lettuce; we will use tomatoes instead.
4. After the terrible meal, the only people left were the host, who was asleep; the waiter, who was cleaning up; and me.
5. Students should use semicolons correctly.

LESSON NOTE: Before you begin this lesson, you might wish to review terms such as *conjunction* and *independent clause*, which were introduced in earlier lessons. Students must be familiar with these terms to master this lesson.

Lesson 40
Colons
1. The time has come: we must dive. The equipment we need is an oxygen tank, a pair of pliers, and a set of hooks. We have rescued people in several states: Florida, Maine, and New York.
2. Students should use colons correctly to separate two main clauses and to introduce a list.

Lesson 41
Apostrophes
1. [no apostrophes]
2. d's; m's; father's
3. Mark's
4. Joni's; women's
5. There's; Meg's; Lans's ideas, who's
6. else's; Lisa's
7. Students should use apostrophes correctly.

COOPERATIVE LEARNING STRATEGY: Many students find it difficult to master the correct use of the apostrophe. You might wish to reinforce this lesson by having small groups either search newspapers for errors in the use of the apostrophe, or compose paragraphs that include apostrophe errors. Then have groups exchange paragraphs and rewrite them so that the apostrophes are used correctly.

Lesson 42
Quotation Marks

1. Jamie said, "Come with me! They're after us!"
2. "Raul said to me, 'I'd like to borrow your science notes.' Then we started talking," Gale said.
3. "Oh, no! They are both gone!" Jack exclaimed. "Now what are we going to do?"
4. Wallis answered, "Nothing. There is nothing we can do."
5. "By the time I got there," Cyndra said, "everyone was still celebrating."
6. Students should use quotation marks correctly.

Lesson 43
Dashes and Parentheses

Answers will vary. Examples:
1. This joking around—as you are aware—must stop immediately.
2. Fun Park (once called Fun World) is on the other side of town.
3. The photographs—pictures of children, of flowers, and of love—stirred deep feelings in us all.
4. I am convinced—correct me if I am wrong—that you are not telling the truth.
5. We ate all the fruit—an orange, an apricot, and a banana.
6. Students should use dashes and parentheses correctly.

Lesson 44
Hyphens

1. pleas-ant
2. choc-o-late
3. for-get-ful-ness
4. vi-ta-mins
5. Students should use hyphens correctly.

Lesson 45
Titles

1. Sidney's book, *The Time to Come*, is based on a short story, "Another Time," which appeared in the magazine *Tomorrow*. Sidney even has plans to make it into a play called *Always Another Time*.
2. Students should use correct punctuation for titles.

Lesson 46
Numbers

1. One thousand students decided to study music in 1980, but only 657 graduated, and of those, only 400 got jobs.
2. [correct]
3. Three hundred forty-five instruments are on display; of those, ninety are violins, thirteen are drums, and fifty-nine are trumpets.
4. Students should write numbers correctly.

Chapter 6
Wrap-Up

1. Answers will vary. Example:
   "Wow! Did Mary tell you what we saw last night?" Heather asked.
   "No," David said. "Maybe you could fill us in."
   "Well, it started when Jack, Pete, and I went to that restaurant last night. It's called The Yellow Hen." Heather said. "We saw Senator Millings—you know, the senator against school funding. He's a friend of my great-aunt."
   "Yes?" David asked.
   "Jack went right up to him and this is what he said," Heather told David.
   "'Senator, have you seen our school? Do you know what shape it's in? Let me tell you how bad it is: The ceilings are leaking, six doors are gone, and the floors are ripped up. What are you going to do about it?' That's what he said."
   "What did the senator do?" David asked.
   "He said he would have a group of fourteen people look into it—I don't know who they would be—and put his administrative aide in charge," Heather said.
2. Students should correctly use mechanics.

Unit 2
What Have You Learned?

1. b
2. b
3. d
4. b
5. a

6. a
7. b
8. a
9. theirs (for *their's*)
10. ? (for the period)
11. none
12. go (for *goes*)
13. I (for *me*)

UNIT NOTE: Terms such as *dependent clause, interjection*, and *conjunction* may intimidate students. Mention to students that names often can give clues to the function of many terms. For example, a dependent clause *depends* on another clause to become a complete sentence. Ask students to think of other examples. (An *independent clause* can "stand alone," an *interjection* "adds information" to a sentence, a *conjunction* "joins" words or phrases.)

To help them review and clarify the terms discussed in this book, direct students to A Guide for Writers: Terms to Know on pages 121–124. This guide also refers students to the page on which each term is taught.

UNIT 3   Analyzing Sentence Style

Unit Opener

1. Students should note that the sentences in Example A seem to flow.
2. Answers will vary.

UNIT NOTE: Advise students that this unit discusses specific ways to make their writing more exciting and more readable. The unit also offers help in showing students how to revise and edit their work. Tell them that the writing skills they are learning will be useful in all of their classes and in their future life. Reports, either for a teacher or for a manager, that are written clearly and with style are apt to receive a more favorable response than those that are written without a clear sense of purpose and audience.

UNIT NOTE: Tell students that they should fill out the first two columns of the chart with what they already know and what they want to learn about

sentences. At the end of the unit, ask students to return to this chart and fill out the third column with what they learned in the unit. You might consider using this chart in individual conferences with students. If students have not learned all of the information they wanted to learn, suggest that they consult the Table of Contents on pages iii–iv or A Guide to Writers: Terms to Know on pages 122–124 for related topics.

Keep in mind that the activities on this page are intended to establish prior knowledge, not to act as a test of information learned. You might consider asking students to return to this page at the end of the unit and to discuss the answers to questions 1 and 2 again, in light of what they learned in their work in the unit. The answers they give before and after completing the unit can serve as an assessment of their learning.

Chapter 7
Varying Sentences

1. Answers will vary. Example:
   Hernando de Soto was one of the most famous gold seekers of all time. He thought there was gold in Florida, and so he went there. De Soto's men feared him and only stayed with him because de Soto told them they would become rich. De Soto drove his men hard, telling them that gold was just ahead. Finally, de Soto fell ill and died near the Mississippi River. He had found no gold.
2. Students should discuss how their revisions made the paragraph more effective.

Lesson 47
Combining Sentences

1. Answers will vary. Example:
   I will never forget the island; I loved it. I remember the white sand and how it sparkled in the sun. When the time came to go, I hid in the bushes so that no one could find me. Then I finally came out, getting on the ship and saying farewell to the island.
2. Students should use a variety of techniques to combine sentences.

COOPERATIVE LEARNING STRATEGY: Give students practice in combining sentences by offering a paragraph of short, simple sentences to small groups of students. Have students create a more interesting paragraph, then have each group read its revision to the class. Each group should also present its reasons for making the revisions it made. You might use this paragraph as a model:

I went to the store. I bought oranges. I bought grapes. I saw a friend. I talked to the friend. He told me some interesting news. I left with my friend. We walked home. We talked. I got home. I had forgotten to buy ground beef for dinner.

Lesson 48
Transition Words
1. however; for example; also; finally
2. Students should have transitions underlined and should be able to discuss how the transitions help their work flow.

Lesson 49
Active and Passive Voice
1. Answers will vary. Example:
   Lamy picked the vegetables. Then, the school chef cooked them. By the time they were served, though, the vegetables had turned to mush. Jim thought that the chef's cooking was terrible. He thought someone should start a petition drive to get a new chef.
2. Students should be able to compare the differences in effectiveness of the active and passive voices.

COOPERATIVE LEARNING STRATEGY: You might wish to bring to class, or have students bring to class, examples of writing that makes extensive use of the passive voice. (Examples can be found in government or technical publications.) Have groups rewrite three or four sentences from these examples in the active voice. Then ask them to discuss the differences in readability and ease of comprehension between the active and passive voices.

Lesson 50
Varying Sentence Beginnings
1. Squawking when they saw anyone approach, the macaws flew around the cage.
2. A normally cheerful man, the trainer was saddened by the death of the gibbon.

3. Unfortunately, the gibbon had been his favorite great ape.
4. Cool and collected, the veterinarian didn't hesitate before he put his hand in the lion's mouth.
5. If they stop jabbering, the monkeys will be let out of their cages in a few minutes.
6. Smiling all the while, the attendant held the doors of the zoo open so that the last visitors could leave.
7. Students should use a variety of sentence beginnings.

ESL/LEP STRATEGY: ESL/LEP students may be confused when they are asked to change the order of words in a sentence. Ask students to work on the questions in this lesson with a proficient English speaker. Have the students complete items 1–6 together, then exchange the work they write for item 7 and critique each other's work.

Chapter 7
Wrap-Up
1. Answers will vary. Example:
   People hike for many different reasons. They like to move their legs, to get exercise, and to see beautiful places. There are so many reasons to hike; however, I can't name them all.
   When I hike, I smell the flowers and breathe the fresh air. I hike to get a different view of the world for a few hours. I am happy and at peace before long, because I know I will feel the good effects for a long time afterward.
2. Students should use the editing techniques discussed in this chapter.

CHAPTER NOTE: Ask students to find writing that excited them or held their attention. Then have students write an analysis of the work by listing and giving examples of the techniques the writer used that are taught in this chapter.

Chapter 8
Building Paragraphs
1. Answers may vary. Example:

Although many people like to buy from mail-order catalogs, there are some problems with doing this. You don't get what you buy right away. The color of the product isn't always the same as what you saw in the catalog. Some catalog companies make returning what you buy difficult. If you're careful and know about these problems, though, you might find that mail-order buying is a good idea for you.

2. Students should discuss the reasons for the changes they made.

Lesson 51
The Paragraph
1. Answers will vary. Example:

   Should you buy a car? There are some good reasons to consider it. One reason is that you can go where you want when you want to go. Another reason is that the sense of freedom you get from having your own car is thrilling.

   There are good reasons, though, to think twice about buying a car. Cars can be very expensive. They can become a magnet for friends who want to borrow them, which means you have to learn to say no to your friends.

   What you have to do is weigh the pros and cons. On the one hand, you have freedom and the knowledge that you don't have to rely on buses or friends for a ride. On the other hand, you have the great expense and worry of having a car. Only you know if buying a car makes sense for you.

2. Students' paragraphs should develop only one idea each.

COOPERATIVE LEARNING STRATEGY: Ask small groups of students to copy three or four paragraphs from a textbook, eliminating the paragraph breaks so that the material appears to be in one paragraph. Then have groups trade these long paragraphs and assign paragraph breaks. Groups can check their work by comparing it to the original source.

Lesson 52
Topic Sentences
Answers will vary. Examples:

1. Television ratings don't protect young children from violent shows.
2. To be successful in school, students must learn to use computers.
3. Basketball is the most exciting sport to watch.

Lesson 53
Supporting Sentences
1. Students should label topic and supporting sentences correctly.
2. Students should construct a paragraph with a topic sentence and sentences that effectively support it.

COOPERATIVE LEARNING STRATEGY: Assign small groups of students the same broad topic (examples include food, holidays, and sports). Then have groups write a paragraph about this topic by creating a topic sentence and supporting sentences. Ask groups to identify each type of supporting sentence they use.

Lesson 54
Organizing Paragraphs
1. Students should correctly label the organizational plan of the paragraph they chose.
2. Students should use two different organizational plans for their paragraphs.

Chapter 8
Wrap-Up
1. Answers will vary. Example:

   Chocolate is made from the seeds of the cacao tree. The seeds grow inside pods on the trees. Then the seeds, or beans, are taken from the pod.

   When they arrive at the factory, the beans are roasted, which brings out their taste. The beans go into huge machines. Then they are ground until they form a dark brown liquid. From there, the chocolate is made into bars and cocoa.

   Chocolate has long been used as a beverage. That was its first use, in fact. When Hernán Cortés came to Mexico, he tasted the drink flavored with cinnamon, sugar, and vanilla, and he loved it. He later brought hot chocolate to Europe, and the drink became popular among the upper classes.

Americans have a love affair with the tropical bean. The United States uses one-fourth of the world's production of cocoa beans in its factories. Chocolate in the United States is very popular in bar form.

2. Students should show an increased understanding of paragraph structure.

CHAPTER NOTE: Impress on students the importance of planning before they write. Point out that many of the errors that occur in paragraph structure would not have occurred if the writer had formed a plan before he or she began to write. You might model this procedure for the class by thinking aloud and making notes on the board. You might choose to write about a topic such as lengthening the school day, or some other topic that will encourage student participation.

Chapter 9
Revising and Editing

1. Answers will vary. Example:

Fireworks were invented in China in the tenth century. Historians think a cook might have mixed together some pickling salts, coal, and sulfur to make a fire. The poor cook found his food exploding. There were few cooks who tried that trick again.

Then the Chinese tried the mixture not as a cooking fuel, but as a rocket. They used these rockets, also called fireworks, to celebrate holidays and weddings. The Chinese called their fireworks "arrows of flying fire."

2. Students should have reasons for their revisions.

CHAPTER NOTE: Begin this chapter by explaining that even professional writers do not turn in a first draft. Professional writers, like students, need to revise and edit their work to make sure they've said exactly what they wish to say.

Lesson 55
Unity

1. Answers will vary. Example:

You have to give up some of your independence when you get a job. You sometimes have to cancel plans because you have to work. You may have to wear a uniform that's embarrassing. Having a job can be a pain.

2. Students should show an understanding of unity.

Lesson 56
Coherence

1. Answers may vary. Example:

You may be surprised to hear how many animals are in the weasel family. Here are three examples. The honey badger, or *Mellivora capensis*, is a member of the weasel family. It lives in Africa and the Middle East. Its skin is so tough it can tear into beehives and not get hurt. *Lutra canadensis* is also a member of the weasel family. It lives in most of the United States and Canada. The *M. vision* is also a weasel. This animal is also called a mink.

2–6. Student self-evaluations should show an understanding of coherence and should point out specific examples of how they achieved it.

Lesson 57
Editing Marks

1. Answers may vary. Example:

Like many inventions, the creation Floating Soap was a mistake the mixer was left on too long. When the soap finished, it had air whipped into it. People loved the new soap because they could find it in their bath tubs when they were taking a bath.

2. Students should use editing marks correctly and should show an understanding of the process of revision.

LESSON NOTE: Editing marks, because they are so widely used, are worth memorizing. Suggest that students commit them to memory for two reasons: they are easy to decipher and they are often used by teachers in higher-level classes. For easy reference, you might also wish to have students flag the page in this lesson that contains the marks. To reinforce their learning, use the marks yourself when you evaluate students' writing.

Lesson 58
Easily Confused Words

1. I felt <u>bad</u> that he lost the race. Then again, <u>it's</u> true that <u>there</u> wasn't much time. To train <u>well</u> for that race, you need more <u>than</u> just ability. You need a good coach and the right diet. <u>Who</u> was going to make sure he was <u>lying</u> down doing his push-ups?
2. Students should use correctly at least six of the easily confused words listed.

ESL/LEP STRATEGY: Easily confused words can be particularly troublesome to ESL/LEP students. Suggest to students that they keep a small notebook dedicated to words that often confuse them, and tell these students to refer to their notebook when they are unsure about a word. They should add to this notebook as they encounter other words that they find confusing.

TEACHING NOTE: Students who are having trouble remembering the difference between easily confused words might consider using index cards as an aid. Have students write the confusing words on one side, and an explanation and example on the other. Suggest that students review their cards whenever they have a few spare minutes

Lesson 59
Spelling

1. If <u>they're</u> going to go, they <u>should</u> remember that there <u>used</u> to be <u>nobody</u> there to give directions.
2. Your <u>piece</u> of pizza has no <u>meat</u> on it.
3. They get their regular, everyday exercise by going to the field, the site of the national <u>championships</u>.
4. There is no <u>reason</u> to sit staring at the <u>ceiling</u>, <u>hoping</u> that you're going to make the team.
5. It <u>may be</u> that they <u>know</u> what they're doing, but I want to give them <u>assistance</u>.
6. In the <u>past</u>, you <u>knew</u> what you <u>were</u> supposed to do.
7. Students should spell and use five troublesome words accurately.

TEACHING NOTE: Although rules are helpful, nothing with regard to spelling is as helpful as a dictionary. Suggest to students that they invest in at least two: one for their backpack at school and another for the location where they normally study.

Also, as with easily confused words, suggest that students make up their own list of spelling words and review it and add to it frequently.

Lesson 60
Spelling Suffixes

1. When Joe <u>dropped</u> the ball, his <u>friend</u> was <u>lying</u> on the ground. That's when the <u>runner</u> ran <u>into</u> Joe. <u>Later</u>, Joe <u>recovered</u>, and the <u>runner</u> <u>tried</u> to help him stand up.
2. Students should add an additional example for each spelling rule.

Lesson 61
Spelling Plurals

1. His deeply held <u>beliefs</u> mean that he never cheats <u>businesses</u>.
2. There are two <u>Russes</u> on the <u>busses</u> that will take us to the <u>rodeos</u>.
3. Usually, he is the first to go to the <u>mailboxes</u>.
4. The three <u>boys</u> had all the <u>radios</u> in their cars, ready to take to <u>parties</u>.
5. Students should show an understanding of the rules of plurals.

Chapter 9
Wrap-Up

1. Answers may vary. Example:
   Have you ever had an ice cream headache? You might have thought it was only in <u>your</u> head. <u>However</u>, <u>scientists</u> who have been <u>studying</u> the ice cream headache say that <u>it's</u> real.
   These <u>scientists</u> found that about 30 percent of people get ice cream <u>headaches</u>. These people eat a spoonful of ice cream and feel a <u>stabbing</u> <u>pain</u> in <u>their</u> face or head. It's a pain that can last for five <u>minutes.</u>
   The <u>scientists</u> who <u>studied</u> these headaches found the <u>answer</u> to the <u>puzzle</u>. They <u>discovered</u> that when the ice cream <u>hits</u> the back of the mouth, it hits the nerves <u>there</u> and <u>causes</u> the <u>headaches</u>. If you want to keep from <u>getting</u> ice cream headaches, just don't gulp ice <u>cream</u> so that it's <u>hitting</u> the back of your mouth.
2. Students should correctly use editing marks and show an understanding of the process of revision.

Unit 3
What Have You Learned?

1. F; passive voice
2. F; *I* is the simple subject
3. F; at the beginning of the paragraph
4. T
5. F; It's
6. none
7. tomatoes
8. lying
9. well
10. receive

UNIT NOTE: Remind students of the importance of editing everything they write. Impress upon them the importance of "getting their ideas on paper" for the first draft, then analyzing the draft to make their ideas clearer and more interesting.

You might also refer students to The Writing Process on page 120 of their book. This page clarifies the steps of the writing process and indicates which activities should be done at each step. Suggest that students commit this process to memory and use it on every piece of writing they produce, not just writing that is assigned. This process will help students clearly say what they want to say.

Student Publications

The possibility of recognition—and even of rewards—can be strong motivations for student writers. The following publications present student writing. Unless otherwise noted, each publication lists guidelines for writers and rules for submission in each issue.

- *The McGuffey Writer*
  McGuffey Foundation School
  5128 Westgate Drive
  Oxford, OH 45056
  513/523-7742
  Intended for readers ages 5–17, *The McGuffey Writer* publishes short stories, essays, poems, plays, and black-and-white artwork from students.

- *Merlyn's Pen: The National Magazines of Student Writing*
  PO Box 1058
  East Greenwich, RI 02818
  401/885-5175
  Merlyn's Pen invites "manuscripts that grip the readers' interest and stir the heart or mind." The emphasis is on the concerns of today's teenagers.

- *Skipping Stones*
  PO Box 3939
  Eugene, OR 97403
  541/342-4956
  Writers through age 18 are strongly encouraged to submit their writing (in any language) and artwork to this bimonthly multicultural magazine.

- *Stone Soup*
  Children's Art Foundation
  PO Box 83
  915 Cedar Street
  Santa Cruz, CA 95063
  408/426-5557
  Stone Soup accepts work from writers through the age of 13. The emphasis of the magazine is on writing and art that is based on personal experiences and observations. A teaching guide in each issue analyzes the selections and offers follow-up activities.

- *Young Author's Magazine/ The Magic Pens*
  140 N. 8th St., Suite 201
  Lincoln, NE 6858
  402/435-2111
  This classroom publication offers monthly issues (of *Young Author's Magazine*) and quarterly anthologies (of *The Magic Pens*) that are devoted to writing by students in grades K–12. Submissions may be in languages other than English. Spanish, French, and Japanese appear often. Priority is given to e-mail submissions at: yam@regulus.com.

Online Publications

- *CyberKids* and *CyberTeens Magazines*
  These online magazines publish student writing and artwork. Send e-mail to cyberkids@mtlake.com. *CyberKids* is on the web at http://www.cyberkids.com/

- *KidPub*
  Another free, online web site, *KidPub* is a home page for readers and writers ages 8–13. Submissions of fiction and nonfiction are posted with brief notes describing the authors. Contact *KidPub* at: http://www.kid-pub.org/kidpub.

- *Slummit*
  The student literary magazine published by Westbury High School in Houston, Texas, this magazine accepts submissions by students. Its web address is: http://slummit@netropolis.net.

Using Graphic Organizers

Graphic organizers are useful tools for helping students organize their thoughts and improve the clarity of their writing. The reproducible masters of graphic organizers on the following pages can be used for any writing assignment in your Language Arts class or in other areas of the curriculum. Here are some ways you can use them:

- Encourage students to use the organizers creatively. Allow students to change or add to an organizer. Students can share their improvements with the rest of the class.

- If a student works more successfully with one kind of organizer than another, you might want to let that student work with that one, regardless of what is suggested on the student page. However, be sure that students try at least one assignment with each organizer.

- Distribute copies of the reproducible masters for students to use when they must write test essays. Allow students to choose the organizers with which they are most comfortable.

- Invite students to evaluate how they use a particular organizer. This may provide insight into the learning styles of your students.

Some lessons require the use of a graphic organizer, though a blank one is not provided in the student book. The students are told to draw the organizer shown on a given page for use with the particular assignment. You may prefer to hand out copies of these reproducible organizers rather than have students hand draw them. Use the following graphic organizers for the lessons noted:

Idea Branch: *Writing to Describe,* page 19

Idea Web: *Writing to Persuade,* page 48

Fact and Opinion Chart: *Writing to Persuade,* pages 49 and 54

Audience Profile Chart 1: *Writing to Persuade,* page 70; *Writing to Describe,* page 69

Audience Profile Chart 2: *Writing to Explain,* page 23; *Writing to Describe,* page 50

Plot Map: *Writing to Explain,* page 26

Outline: *Writing to Explain,* page 26

Chain of Events: *Writing to Explain,* page 26

Apply It

▶ Use this idea branch to explore and focus your ideas for your letter. Write your response in the center circle. Add your reasons. Then add facts to support the reasons. Add more circles if you need them. Then choose the most important reason and the most important facts to support it.

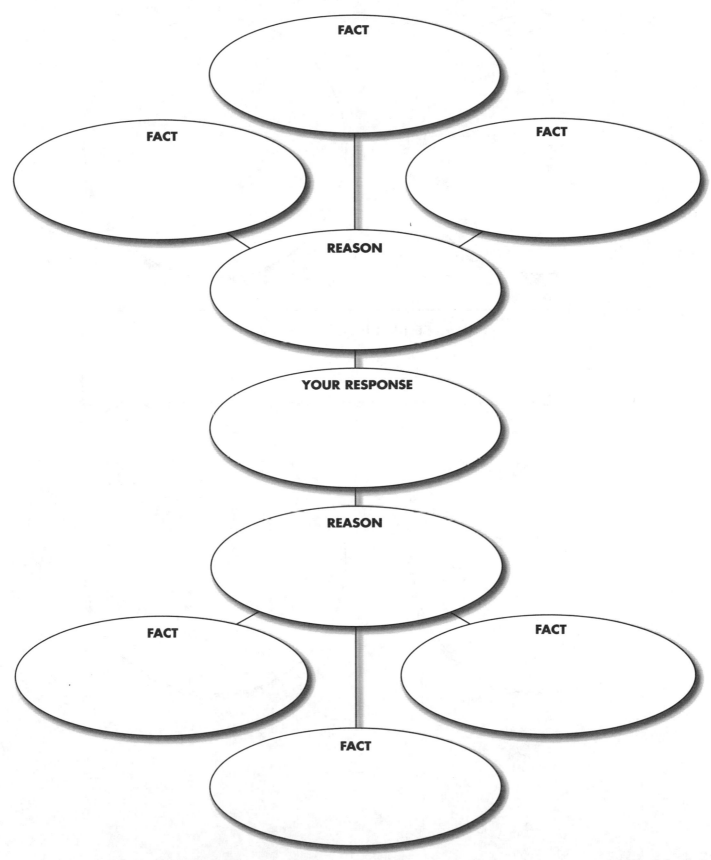

Idea Web

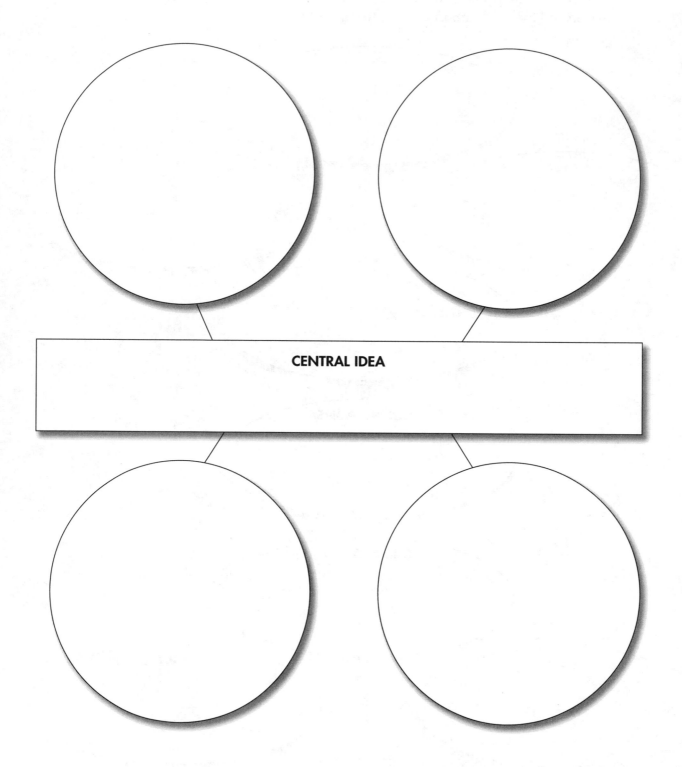

CENTRAL IDEA

Fact and Opinion Chart

Topic

Opinions	Facts, Reasons, Examples

Audience Profile Chart 1

TOPIC:	
AUDIENCE:	
AUDIENCE NEEDS TO KNOW	**DETAILS TO MATCH AUDIENCE NEEDS**

Audience Profile Chart 2

NARROWED TOPIC:
AUDIENCE:
AGE RANGE/POSITION:
KNOWLEDGE REGARDING TOPIC:
OTHER FACTS THEY MAY NEED TO KNOW:
INTERESTS REGARDING TOPIC:

Plot Map

RISING ACTION:	CLIMAX:

CONFLICT:	RESOLUTION:

Outline

. . . . Outline ▪ ▪ ▪

FIRST EVENT   I. _____

      DETAIL   A. _____

      DETAIL   B. _____

NEXT EVENT   II. _____

      DETAIL   A. _____

      DETAIL   B. _____

NEXT EVENT   III _____

      DETAIL   A. _____

      DETAIL   B. _____

NEXT EVENT   IV _____

      DETAIL   A. _____

      DETAIL   B. _____

LAST EVENT   V. _____

      DETAIL   A. _____

      DETAIL   B. _____

Chain of Events

EVENT:
TIME:
NOTES:

EVENT:
TIME:
NOTES:

EVENT:
TIME:
NOTES:

EVENT:
TIME:
NOTES:

EVENT:
TIME:
NOTES:

FINISH

Student Self-Assessment Form

Name _____

Unit _____ Chapter _____

The following questions will help you focus your writing.
Before you begin a chapter, fill in the following:
1. What is my goal in this chapter?

_____

_____

_____

2. What questions do I want to ask before I begin writing?

_____

_____

_____

After you complete an essay, fill in the following:
1. What is the purpose of my essay? Did I state it clearly and support it well throughout?

_____

_____

2. Did I present my reasons and facts in a logical manner? If not, how can I improve the organization?

_____

_____

3. How can I improve my use of sufficient and interesting supporting details?

_____

_____

4. How was my use of grammar, punctuation, and spelling?

_____

_____

After you finish the chapter, fill in the following:
1. How well have I met my goal?

_____

_____

2. With what areas did I have problems? With what areas did I have the most success?

_____

_____

_____

3. What could I have done to better meet my goal?

_____

_____

_____

Peer-Assessment Checklist

Name of Writer _____

Name of Evaluator _____

Unit _____ Chapter _____

Use this checklist to help you evaluate the writing of your classmate. A 5 is the highest rating and a 1 is the lowest.

Areas	Rating	Comments and Examples
Content		
■ Is the content of the writing thoughtful and accurate? ■ Is the topic narrow enough? ■ Does the introduction catch the reader's attention? ■ Does the introduction tell the point of the essay? ■ Is there a clear main idea throughout the essay? ■ Is the content right for the audience and purpose? ■ Is there evidence and detail to support the main idea? ■ Does the conclusion contain a restatement of the main idea? ■ Is the essay interesting? **Organization** ■ Is the content organized logically and effectively? ■ Do all the ideas and details support the key point? ■ Do the points flow smoothly from one to the other? **Proofreading** ■ Is the writing clear? Do the sentences make sense? ■ Are the sentences varied in length and structure? ■ Is the essay free of grammar, punctuation, and spelling errors?		

Writing Assessment: Writing to Persuade

The following two essays are examples of persuasive writing. These essays were written in response to the question below. Essay A is well written. Essay B needs improvement. Read both essays. Then answer the questions.

Should all students have to take gym class? Write an essay that gives your opinion.

Essay A:

All students should have to take gym class. Exercise is important to staying healthy. It has been proven that people who exercise live longer, healthier lives. For much of the school day, students sit in their chairs. Thus, gym class is the only chance most students have to exercise.

Some might argue that not everyone is athletic. They think that these students should not be forced to participate in sports. Not all students are good at writing, either. However, all students are required to take English every year. The only way that a person will improve, either at writing or at sports, is to practice.

All students benefit from taking gym class. The healthy exercise habits students learn as teenagers will stay with them throughout their lives.

Essay B:

I think that every student should take gym class. Gym class is fun and good for you. Most students are too serious. They spend all day in class learning things like math and English. Then they have to do homework and study after school. Gym class lets them have fun. They get to play games like baseball and go swimming.

Gym is good for students. We all need to exercise. No one wants to be overweight.

1. What makes Essay A a good example of persuasive writing?

_____

_____

_____

_____

_____

2. What suggestions do you have to improve Essay B?

_____

_____

_____

_____

_____

Writing Assessment: Writing to Tell a Story

The following two essays are examples of narrative writing. The essays were written in response to the instructions below. Essay A is well written. Essay B needs improvement. Read both essays. Then answer the questions.

Write an essay that tells a story about a time when you helped someone. Show what you learned from that experience.

Essay A:

Every weekend, I spend my evenings delivering meals to people who can't leave their homes. I'll never forget the first person I ever visited. She was a ninety-year-old woman named Emma.

Emma lives by herself and needs to use a wheelchair. At first, I was afraid to talk to her. Then Emma began telling me the most awful jokes. They were so bad, I couldn't help but laugh. She and I began talking. I must have stayed for at least two hours that first day.

I continue to visit her every weekend. I look forward to our visit and our talks. Emma tells me fascinating stories about her childhood, her world travels, and what it's like to grow older. She also gives me wonderful advice.

Helping others does make me feel good about myself. However, becoming friends with someone so much older and wiser has helped me more than I ever could have imagined.

Essay B:

Once, I volunteered to teach younger students how to read better. I worked with a young girl who read very slowly. She couldn't sound out a lot of the words.

At first, her slowness annoyed me. Then I spent a lot of time helping her learn all the sounds of the letters and words. She started to read faster. I learned to be patient.

1. What makes Essay A a good example of narrative writing?

_____

_____

_____

_____

_____

2. What suggestions do you have to improve Essay B?

_____

_____

_____

_____

_____

Writing Assessment: Writing to Explain

The following two essays are examples of expository writing. The essays were written in response to the instruction below. Essay A is well written. Essay B needs improvement. Read both essays, then answer the questions.

Write an essay summarizing a short story you have read.

ESSAY A:

The Secret Life of Walter Mitty is a short story by James Thurber. It tells about Walter, who is always daydreaming. When he daydreams, Walter doesn't pay attention to what he's doing.

First, Walter daydreams that he is piloting a hydroplane through a hurricane. His wife yells at him for driving too fast. You find out he is really driving his wife to the beauty parlor.

Next, he daydreams he's a world famous surgeon saving a millionaire patient. This dream ends when a parking-lot attendant yells at him for driving in the wrong lane.

Another time, Walter goes shopping. He buys overshoes and begins to imagine that he is a murder suspect on the witness stand. Suddenly, he realizes that he has forgotten to buy dog biscuits.

Walter then goes to meet his wife. While waiting, he daydreams about being a fighter pilot. Walter comes out of it when his wife yells at him for being hard to find. The story ends with Walter waiting for his wife outside a drugstore. He imagines he's facing a firing squad!

Essay B:

The short story I read was by Ray Bradbury. Its about a house left standing after a bomb kills all the people.

The house is mechanical. It makes breakfast even though no one is there. It does a lot of other things automatically. Then a tree falls and starts a fire. The fire destroys the whole house except for one wall. The mechanical voice in the wall keeps repeating the date.

1. What makes Essay A a good example of expository writing?

_____

_____

_____

_____

_____

2. What suggestions do you have to improve Essay B?

_____

_____

_____

_____

_____

Writing Assessment: Writing to Describe

The following two essays are examples of descriptive writing. The essays were written in response to the instructions below. Essay A is well written. Essay B needs improvement. Read both. Then answer the questions.

Write an essay to describe a pet. Describe any reasons why the pet is important to you.

Essay A

The first thing most people say when they meet my dog, Bobo, is "What is that?" Bobo is a mix of fox terrier, Chihuahua, boxer, and a few other breeds we can't identify.

Bobo weighs about 15 pounds and is only a foot tall at the shoulders. He has short, stubby legs. I like that he's small so he can sit on my lap.

Bobo has a pug nose, like someone squished his face. Tufts of long, light brown fur stick out of the top of his head. The rest of his head looks almost bald. Its covered with a yellowy white fuzz. The hair on his body is the same color, but a little longer. To me, his fur feels like velvet.

Bobo looks unusual, but he's very lovable. Whenever I'm upset, he climbs into my lap and licks my hand or face. He sleeps in my room every night. He makes me happy just by being there.

Essay B:

I like my cat Milo. He's a pretty cat. He is an Angora. This kind of cat has long hair. Milo has white, long hair. Some Angora cats have brown eyes. Some have green ones and some have blue. Milo has blue eyes.

Milo is big and heavy. But he lets me pick him up and carry him around if I want to. I have to brush him a lot. I like Milo because he's nice.

1. What makes Essay A a good example of descriptive writing?

_____

_____

_____

_____

_____

2. What suggestions do you have to improve the Essay B?

_____

_____

_____

_____

_____